Joyce Herzog's

CHOOSING & USING
CURRICULUM
Your Guide to Home Education

CURRICULUM TYPES
HOMESCHOOL STYLES
BACK TO BASICS
SNAPSHOT OF PROGRESS
AND MORE!

- Get a Right Start!
- Reading Comprehension
- Written Expression
- Christian Perspective
- Snapshot of Progress
- Discernment
- Adapting Material
- Resources
- Special Education Resources, too!

©Joyce M. Herzog 1994, 2001
Published by

Joyce Herzog.com
http://www.joyceherzog.com
800-745-8212

ISBN Number: 1-887225-22-6

Table of Contents

About the Author:

Joyce Herzog is a Christian educator, author, consultant, and speaker. She has a master's degree and 25 years experience in teaching students with learning disabilities. Her background includes teaching, evaluating, choosing curriculum, as well as planning and implementing programs for individuals and schools. She has been consulting for more than ten years with homeschooling families and is the author of *The Scaredy Cat Reading System, History in His Hands Series, Luke's List, Learning in Spite of Labels,* the *Stepping Stones Series of Family Devotions* and much more.

Joyce started her teaching career in second grade, where she helped fellow students understand what the teacher did not make clear. She decided to be a teacher then, and years later earned a Bachelor's Degree in education. Later, when learning disabilities (LD) emerged into a special field, Joyce earned a Master's Degree in LD from the University of Iowa. Her writings merited her an honorary doctorate in Humane Letters from the Jacksonville Theological Seminary. She has pioneered programs and taught special education and an LD curriculum in several states, and holds a permanent teacher's certificate in the state of Iowa with an LD endorsement. She is listed in *Who's Who In American Education.* Though only a few years old, her *Scaredy Cat Reading System* is used in over 40 states to teach gifted children as well as those who can't seem to learn by any other system. Her book, *Learning in Spite of Labels,* has enjoyed enthusiastic acceptance and proved to be a blessing to many families in their search for a better way of educating their children. It offers techniques that can be used to good advantage in any teaching situation and presents a Christian perspective of education. She has developed many other educational products which may be seen in the internet at www.joyceherzog.com.

Author's Note

As you begin this awesome task of choosing the curriculum which will shape your future and your child's life, take a look at who he is, who he can become, and what God's call on his life is. Be willing to adapt to your child's needs. Concentrate on his abilities rather than his disabilities. If he has no hands, teach him to play soccer! If he has four hands, teach him to juggle!

Give your student some control over his own life. Listen to him. He may have the best idea about how he can learn or express to you what he has learned! Do not spend more than half of your time remediating a weakness. You must allow him to experiment and have experiences in many different areas to discover his strengths. Always encourage him to do his best, but always accept his best effort. Do not ask the impossible. Do not expect him to fail. Expect him to give it his best shot no matter what it is! Praise all real accomplishments. Praise all steps toward maturity. Don't coddle him, he'll need strength of character to cope with his weakness!

Chapter One

Introduction

**Choosing Curriculum for any child
is not an impossible task.**

Here are some important things to consider:
Most children need **systematic** (orderly), **incremental** (bite-sized) lessons **relevant** to their lives and taught in a **comfortable multi-sensory** (using several senses) environment. Practice should involve all of the child - seeing, saying, and writing is not enough. It must also **"grab" his interest** and, when possible, his **funny bone**, his **sensitive spirit,** his sense of **rhythm**, and his whole **body in movement.** This is particularly important in teaching the skill of reading. Whenever possible he needs to see the **big picture** first and all pieces of the puzzle should be related to the big picture or other known information. Information should be taught within a **relevant context.** Special learners need **adequate space** to write answers - short answers which require little copying and minimal written response. They, in particular need **alternate methods of responding** especially when written skills are minimal or not in keeping with mental ability.

We have all been indoctrinated into an academic, grade level, take twelve-years-to-learn-little mentality. Our first job is to look at what we are teaching, why we are teaching it, and whether it is in God's design for us to do it. Do not let the world pour you into its mold! If the schools were succeeding, they would be a good model to follow, but what are they succeeding at? Most are succeeding in developing cattle with neither skills nor character sufficient to think, evaluate, or revolt! If it works, send them there; if it doesn't, don't import it!

It is first of all important that you determine what you want to teach, what values you want to pass on, and whether your child at the end of the process you are planning will be prepared for anything beyond one more year of school. These are some very important foundational questions most of us have been ignoring. This book and my other book *Learning In Spite of Labels* help you look at these and more questions and work toward cleansing your thinking of the secular bias learned from television and public education.

Once you get beyond these basic issues, here are some basic questions to ask when looking at any curriculum – especially important for our unique or struggling learners:

- Are the pages cluttered?
- Is there enough room for your student to do the work and write the answers?
- Are the concepts presented first of all in a concrete way (with real objects), then in a transition (pictures of objects), then in symbols?
- Are the skills taught in small enough steps for your student to understand and make progress?
- Is there adequate practice in a variety of skills to achieve mastery?
- Is there a clear-cut way to determine mastery so you know when to introduce a new topic?
- Is the presentation conducive to transfer of information to the real world?
- Is there a multi-sensory presentation which involves all of the learner - body (the five senses), soul (intellect, will, emotions), spirit (deeper nature)?
- Does the curriculum allow the flexibility to involve your whole family?
- Will the curriculum fall apart if you are ill or miss a week's lessons?

When you attend a book fair or homeschooling convention, there are some other questions you may want to ask the vendors:

• "Did you write this material?" There are many authors who are basically introverts and do not come out and hound you. They have written these materials based on their own experience and may save you years of "hard knocks learning" if you tap into their wisdom.

• If they say yes, ask: "Why did you write this?" Their answer will reveal their heart and some very important things about their philosophy and whether it agrees with your own.

• If they say no, ask: "Have you ever used it?" If they answer, "Yes," ask what they liked best about it and what they disliked most about it. They may say, "I loved the way it told me exactly what to say and do every day," and you may respond with "Yea!" or "Ycch!" Either way you've learned something about the program **and** you've solidified your own preferences.

Another hint for attending those conventions: Go at least 2 days if at all possible. The first day, go through the exhibit hall with lots of questions. Ask. Listen. Look. Take notes. Go back to ones that stick in your mind. **But don't buy!** Go back home (or to your motel) and let it all sink in. Look over brochures and catalogs you've picked up. **Pray!** Then go back the next day to the things that really stick in your mind and heart. Make informed careful decisions. You'll still make mistakes, but they'll be fewer and less costly.

It is not necessary, nor probably even desirable, to stick with a single textbook curriculum. Textbooks are seldom delightful for reluctant learners and if your student isn't enjoying learning, you won't enjoy teaching! Be willing to try new methods and new materials. If something doesn't work for you, sell it at a used curriculum fair to someone who can profit from it, and try something else!

Note: Throughout the book, companies are bold and underlined, individual products are bold and italicized. Products which do not have an address are commonly available from the major homeschool distributors such as The Elijah Company, Lifetime Books and Gifts, and Timberdoodle.

Chapter Two

Curriculum Types and Comments

Four basic types to be contrasted here are **Textbook, Workbook, Directed Unit Study** and **Real Books** approach. Each has built in advantages and disadvantages with some special significance for special needs students. See the charts on the following page for comparisons.

Textbooks such as *Bob Jones University, ABeka, Rod and Staff, What Every First (Second, etc.) Grader Should Know,* provide information to be read, studied and tested. Response to texts is usually on separate paper and may require copying of problems or questions before doing the work. Typical procedure is for the teacher to introduce the topic, the student to read a chapter and then take a test. These tend to emphasize memorization of facts.

Workbook such as *Accelerated Christian Education (A.C.E.), BASIC, Alpha Omega, First (Second, etc.) Grade Yearbooks,* and *Simplified Curriculum* give information in small bites and permit writing the answer directly in the workbook. Typical procedure is for the student to read and fill in the blanks. They tend to emphasize immediate recall of facts.

Modified or Directed Unit Study such as *ATIA, Weaver, Konos, Alta Vista Curriculum, Tapestry,* and the *Prairie Primer* vary considerably from the very active and largely hands-on (Konos) to studies centered around the Bible (Weaver and ATIA) or a series of books (Prairie Primer) to a more loosely connected and more application-centered style (Alta Vista). The procedure is for the teacher to prepare by reading and gathering what is needed and then leading the students through the study as they read, make things, do things, discuss, and take trips. Most of the suggestions for the activities are included in the material, which is purchased.

Unit Study or Real Books Approach makes use of a wide variety of resources and many real books to expose the student to many approaches and materials within the context of a single topic around which all the subjects are centered. The topic may be chosen by the teacher or suggested by the students or grow out of a book read, a trip taken, a question or interest of a students, a curriculum guide (such as World Book Encyclopedia puts out) or scope and sequence from a major curriculum. General procedure is for an introduction to the topic to be followed by reading books (aloud by teacher and individually by student), doing activities related to the topic, taking field trips, and some kind of a project. Pictures are often taken of activities and projects, and students record what they have learned in various other ways. Much use is made of real books, research techniques, discussion, interviewing experts, videos and other means of learning about the topic.

Textbook

Advantages	Disadvantages	Special Needs
Easy to follow	Cumbersome to manage	Often have difficulty transferring learning to life
"Everything" provided	Very expensive	Copying from book (especially in math) may be counterproductive
Colorful	Time consuming	
Teacher's manuals provide adequate learning suggestions	Difficult or impossible to manage several grade levels	
Durable	The more children, the less real teaching and teacher involvement	
"Covers" all subjects at all grade levels	Designed for classroom use, requires modification for individual use	
	May become the controller	

How to use textbooks for best results:

• Use textbooks as a tool.

• Use for one subject for several children in the same book.

• Two or three grade levels of children may be able to work from the same text for such subjects as history or science.

• The upper level texts in history, science and literature may be used for reference much like an encyclopedia.

• May need to be modified for math as it is unproductive for a reluctant learner to spend half or more of his math class copying problems.

Workbook

Advantages	Disadvantages	Special Needs
Straightforward	Makes possible filling in blanks without thinking or learning	Transfer of learning to "real" situations is minimal
Easy to manage		Seems to put emphasis on finishing rather than learning
Little preparation	No choices to make	
Child works independently	Leads to minimal teaching and teacher involvement	Does not allow for different learning styles
Structured		
Gives teacher security	Minimal accountability	Does not allow for different or divergent thinking
Budget effective for one child	May encourage cheating	Requires much writing, though less than texts
Diagnostic and can place child at his ability level in different subjects	Parent may become manager rather than teacher	
Can carry on without teacher present	Structure and lack of variety may lead to lack of creativity and enjoyment	
Initially increases confidence of teacher and student	Some do not provide enough repetition – others too much	
"Covers" all subjects at all grade levels	Expensive for several children	

How to use workbooks for best results:

Choose a subject or two each year to concentrate on **really** teaching and allow the student to do workbooks in one or more of the other subjects. You may wish to spend a year really concentrating on developing character qualities and Bible knowledge and math skills through manipulatives, demonstrations, discussions and application. For that year, a workbook approach may be used for history, science and language arts. Another year you may choose to concentrate on developing written language through the content areas of science, history and Bible. During that year, maintain math skills through workbooks. Use workbooks as a tool to simplify your life and maintain skills. If you are a hodge-podge activity-and-project oriented person, use one of the yearbooks to provide some structure and ensure no gaps in learning.

Directed Unit Study

Advantages	Disadvantages	Special Needs
Permits multi-level learning Gives structure without limiting creativity Very life related Usually very hands on Encourages creativity Gives teacher many suggestions while allowing much flexibility	Does not include math, reading, or basic grammar instruction Choices are required Usually need many resources or much use of library Dependent on health and presence of teacher	Very adaptable to different levels and learning styles There is almost always some activity that fits each student

How to use for best results:

These are usually designed to be used over a period of time and cover nearly every subject.

If you stick with one system, you are likely to cover important material in every field.

If you change styles and approaches every year, this will probably be the hardest to move in and out of.

If you need a break from textbooks or workbooks but still require structure and direction, try this out!

Real Books

Advantages	Disadvantages	Special Needs
Permits multi-level learning	Requires much preparation	Very adaptable to different levels and learning styles
Usually very hands on	Requires decision making	Easy to give purpose and carry-over of learning
Develops research skills	Overwhelming to those who need structure	
Encourages creativity	Intimidates the insecure	
High parent involvement	Need variety of research materials available	
Encourages learning together		
Freedom for creativity	Initially very dependent on the teacher	
Flexibility in planning	May be "hit-or-miss" in covering topics	
Easy adjustment for interest and ability of individual	Does not include math, reading or basic grammar instruction	
Materials reusable for other family members.	Usually need resources or much use of a good library	

How to use real books for best results:

- Occasionally break the monotony of textbook or workbook approaches with a unit study. Do a unit study for a week to a month and then return to your other approach for a week to a month.

- Have a unit study which incorporates all subjects except reading and math instruction.

- Allow the older learners to choose and lead a unit study.

Bonus Box

Autism

Autism is an issue which needs a totally different approach from many special needs. Early identification is essential for good progress. Autism is just beginning to be understood and still neither cause nor cure has been identified. On the other hand, identification of the syndrome, clues to how the brain works, and some positive interventions are giving new hope.

Autism is a brain disorder that typically affects a person's ability to communicate, form relationships with others, and respond appropriately to the environment. It is a cluster of behaviors affecting language, communication, emotional, cognitive, behavioral and both fine and gross motor skills. It often seems to develop during the toddler years, is far more prevalent in boys than girls, and presently affects approximately 1 in 500 children.

Act early: If your young child doesn't respond emotionally or to simple verbal directions, pretend, point to objects named, or seems to live in "his own world' and is upset by normal sensory stimulation or change, seek professional attention.

Educate yourself: Read books, surf the web, talk to others. Don't panic. Find out as much as you can. Be a part of the solution for your family and others.

Work with your child: Devise routines that help him gain control. Teach step by step skills such as interpreting facial expressions, how to share and make friends, and other appropriate social behaviors that come automatically to most of us.

Work as a family: Do not take your frustrations out on your family. Love and support each individual. Get respite help to keep your marriage intact. Give each child attention and a voice in expressing and solving problems.

Keep a sense of humor: Find ways to laugh at the uniqueness of your child and his approach to life. Find humor in tiny successes and even in failed attempts. Enjoy your child.

Notice progress: Celebrate each small step of progress. Take a fifteen-minute video of your child twice a year. Jot down little steps of progress. Ask friends to point out progress they see.

Network: Find ways to communicate with others who are further along than you and others who can learn from your experience. Both help you keep your perspective.

Plan ahead: Your child will need a support system in the event of your death. Having a plan in place **before** it is needed comforts all.

See also chart on page 78 for more about autism.

Chapter Three
Which One Is Me?

How do you decide which curriculum is best for you? Well, be assured it will take some trial and error. Most of those who are reading this book have been educated "in the system." We were either schooled in a public or private school – an institutional setting. That is the only thing we have to refer to when we decide to homeschool. Our natural inclination is to set up our "school" exactly like the school we attended. We buy our stacks of textbooks and every workbook and teacher's manual and extra supplement that is suggested. Then we add a few of those "wonderful looking" new materials with "hands-on," "multi-sensory," or other new-fangled catchy come-on. Then we get home, spread it all out on the floor, and wonder what in the world to do with it and where to start. After a year, or two or three, we are burned out and wonder why we ever got into this in the first place. We consider sending our children back to "real school," begin to think of this experience as a failed experiment, and see ourselves as a failure as well.

Many are worried that a child will "miss something." Let me put those fears to rest. I assure you that your child **will** miss something! Everyone does! We all have gaps in our learning. Yet we all manage to learn what we need to when we need to. God isn't through with any of us yet! Not even a PERFECT teacher (if there is such a thing) can "cover everything." Decisions have to be made along the way as to what is **most** important **at this time** with a constant vigilance toward the long term future – adulthood. Think about your goals. Do you want your child to cover a curriculum, master certain skills, be prepared to reenter the "system" at some grade level, be prepared for life, learn to love God, love learning, or "all of the above?" You can't do EVERYTHING!

One thing is certain. The more time and prayer you put into the decision **before** you begin homeschooling, the more comfortable you will be. Do your homework. Go to homeschool conventions. Visit teacher supply stores. Look at a wide variety of materials. Talk to others who are homeschooling. Get to know your children. Do the "Take A Snapshot of Your Child's Progress!" from Chapter Nine. Try to determine the grade level of your children's reading, writing and math using achievement tests or the next chapter's simple outline.

Take a look at the following descriptions to see which type of homeschool you are thinking of creating. That will give you a good idea of what type of materials you will want to purchase. Please remember, as different as they are, all are valid approaches to homeschooling. No one style is appropriate for every homeschool. Some families will need to choose one method for one child and a different way for others. Be flexible. Be willing to adapt, change, and abandon what doesn't work. When the Bible says, "Train up a child in the way he should go," it implies that the same approach is not right for everyone! Remember, your approach to curriculum will grow out of your personality, your life philosophy, and the unique traits of the children God has put in your family!

Homeschool Styles

Mrs. High Performance Homeschooler recreates the public school at home. The walls are filled with alphabets and maps. The children sit in desks or at tables with stacks of textbooks. At nine o'clock five days a week, the children appear dressed and polished. Their beds are made, their chores are done, their hair is combed, their breakfast is eaten (and cleaned up after), they carry their homework to their desk, wait for all to say the pledge, and (perhaps) open with prayer and Bible. Mrs. High Performance has graded yesterday's work and planned for today. She knows just what page each child is on in every book and how many pages they must complete today in order to be finished by the end of the school year which is laid out according to the plan of her local school. The children know what they are expected to do and are able to determine for themselves when they are finished for the day.

Mrs. Happy Homeschooler is less structured. In fact there is no structure. The children have gone to bed at various times of their own choosing and rise in the morning when they want. They fix and eat their own breakfast (if they want it at all). By eleven o'clock, everyone is usually moving. Susie has read a book silently, Johnny is digging a hole in the back yard, Mark is (as usual) playing with his Legos™, and the baby's diaper still needs changing. After a while, Susie has a great idea, "Let's go to the beach and dig for clams." Everyone agrees and they pack peanut butter and jelly sandwiches and head for the beach. On the way home, they stop at the library to get some books about clams and a video about the four seasons. Right before supper, Mom panics, realizing that they haven't done any math or writing today. She gathers all the kids together, assigning them to figure out how many miles they drove, how long it took, how much gas they used, and how much cheaper it would have been if they had all had motorcycles. They each write their findings and hand it to Dad as he comes home. They school year round, or not at all according to some observers.

Mrs. Hopeful Homeschooler is somewhere in between. She plans to spend 2 to 3 hours each morning in "table time." During that time, she supervises each school-age child in reading, writing, copywork, and math while the older ones take turns caring for and working with the little ones. Later, the older ones make lunch while she cuddles and reads to the little ones. After lunch, she reads to the older children or they work together on a unit study while the little ones are napping. After nap, she puts in a few loads of laundry and has playtime with the little ones while the older ones work on homework - usually projects - which have been assigned in the morning. By three or four o'clock, everyone is finished and free for the remainder of the day. After supper, Daddy takes time to play with the children and tries to talk with each child about what they have done while mother plans the next day.

Mrs. Average Homeschooler (a Hopeful wannabe) has four children, approximately two years apart. All are different and have noticeable strengths and differences. She is convinced that the public school does NOT know what is best for her children but is not convinced that she does, either. Her teaching style is an eclectic mix of unit studies, literature based unit studies, Charlotte Mason, and classical education sprinkled with an occasional "unschool" day of games and pursuing the child's own interest. She tries to schedule her days but often finds that the schedule goes out the window due to an emergency, an exceptionally good book, or the fact that the kids find a butterfly, decide to examine it under the microscope, then draw it and end up making a "butterfly museum." Sorting socks counts as a pre-reading activity and making a weekly quadruple batch of M&M cookies counts as math.

Her home is never as clean as she would like and there is always another pile of laundry to fold. Her kitchen table doubles as a school desk, art center and often finds itself (to her horror) holding tadpoles or frogs or the tiny pieces of whatever old appliance the boys are currently taking apart. She has at least one bookcase in every room in the house, including closets, and still needs more room for school stuff. She is always looking for ways to cut back on the grocery budget, and ends up spending the money on books. Houseplants are considered an endangered species, but at least her **children** are growing. Her idea of a good reading is "Little House on the Prairie," and she reads and re-reads books on home education as well as some of her favorite homeschool catalogs. Her friends either think she's a saint who never loses her patience (HA! HA! What they don't see!) or that she's just plain crazy. Her in-laws would prefer that their grandchildren went to public school but are usually polite enough not to say so.

After a day of reading to her children, teaching them to read, teaching them letters and numbers, math, fractions, decimals, science, history, Latin and Greek root words, nature study, painting, drawing, manners, how to sweep, cook and clean, how to take apart the VCR **and** put it back together, how to love others and to see how the Lord shows His Love for them, she lays down at night exhausted and wonders "Did we do enough today?"

Mrs. Troubled Young Homeschooler has only two children. Jasper is a toddler and Origami is in Kindergarten. She is often tired and needs to nap whenever Jasper naps. Every day she tries to squeeze in a few minutes for school with Origami, but often she only manages to read aloud whatever book Origami brings to her. She already dreads the day when Origami turns seven and the state "demands" that she "keep records" and spend four hours a day in "school."

Mrs. Terrific First Year Homeschooler has one preschooler. She has an immaculate house which takes little time to maintain and devotes all her time to her precocious little one. She has a carefully maintained Memory Album from the moment she knew the little one was on his way. She wakes every day eager to spend time with all the activities she's chosen for their time together. Take a break for summer? She wouldn't think of it; she'll just change to a shorter day, more relaxed activities, and add in some swimming lessons.

Mrs. Houseful Homeschooler has seventeen children: two teens and ten under seven years of age. Nine are adopted. Seven have special needs, six are in diapers and one is on a feeding tube. Among the diagnoses are ADD, ADHD, Tourette's Syndrome, Autism, Cerebral Palsy, Down's Syndrome, and Fetal Alcohol Syndrome. A lady in her church who was closing out a small preschool donated all her equipment and toys which are all over the place. She is content to be doing what the Lord has called her to, but wonders how she can do it all every day. They live on a farm and are very involved in nurturing and caring for the garden and animals. Every day is "school" and no day is just like any other. Lessons come up as they are needed, teaching Johnny and Elizabeth to tie their shoes, Susie and Sam to count the plates and silverware as they set the table, and Mark and Rob to write a thank you letter to Grandma for their new jackets. She makes sure the children are read to every day either by herself or one of the older ones and that those who can, are taught to read and do basic math, and figures they'll catch up with everything else when they can do it on their own.

Mrs. "I Don't Know What to DO with Johnny" Homeschooler has one (or two) children who have every label known to man. They are learning disabled, ADHD, gifted, emotionally disturbed and have autistic tendencies. In other words, the world does not know what to do with them and neither does Mrs. "I Don't Know What To Do." She is looking for the "sixth grade learning disability curriculum," but doesn't know what company makes it. There are other children in the home, but they are all learning and working independently and not a problem to be considered.

Practical Curriculum Suggestions for Each:

Mrs. High Performance Homeschooler will want to look at the "big boy" publishers who handle a full curriculum at all grade levels. She will be most comfortable with a textbook or workbook curriculum. She will know what the children are doing and be sure that they have "covered" the curriculum. Some of the "Big Boys" are:

Abeka Book Publications • 800-874-2352
A.C.E. School of Tomorrow • 800-876-6176
AlphaOmega LifePac • 800-821-4443
Bob Jones University Press • 800-845-5731
Christian Liberty Press • 708-259-8736
Christian Light • 540-434-0750
Rod and Staff • 606-522-4348
Saxon Math sold by many homeschool retail stores.

Mrs. Happy Homeschooler will want to live near a library to jump into those last minute unit studies. She may want a hands-on approach to reading and math. She might be helped by a list of books to encourage her children to read (Beautiful Feet, Sonlight Curriculum or Honey for a Child's Heart). Educational toys and placemats and magazines mailed directly to the children might be a good idea. She, in particular, would find an all-inclusive list like *Luke's School List* helpful as her children enter the junior high years to allow them to check for themselves what they have learned or may be missing.
Curricula for Mrs. Happy to look at include:
Math: *MathUSee, Making Math Meaningful, Mastering Mathematics*
Reading: *Scaredy Cat Reading System, Sing Spell, Read and Write*
School in a Box • 800-745-8212
Backyard Scientist • P. O. Box 16966 • Irvine, CA 92713
God's World Magazine • P.O. Box 2330 • Asheville, NC 28802-2330 • 800-951-5437
Guideposts for Kids • 16 East 34th St. NY, NY 10016 • FAX 914-228-2151 • 800-932-2145
Ranger Rick Magazine • 8925 Leesburg Pike • Vienna, VA 22184-0001 • 800-432-6564
Nature Friend Magazine • 2673 TR421 • Sugarcreek, OH 44681 • 800-852-4482

Mrs. Hopeful Homeschooler may choose from a variety of materials. She is likely to want a math program and a book or curriculum to teach her young one to read. For the other subject areas, she may choose a unit-study type of curriculum or pull together her own ideas. She may

use very different materials each year thinking that eventually she will "cover" everything by having done so much over so many years. She, in particular, would find an all-inclusive list like *Luke's School List* helpful as her children enter the junior high years to allow them to check for themselves what they have learned or may be missing. *Luke's School List* would also benefit her as a guide for the K-6 years and a checklist to be used by each student as they enter junior high.
Luke's School List and *School in a Box* by Joyce Herzog • 800-745-8212
Modified Unit Study; *Weaver, Konos, Alta Vista, Prairie Primer, Tapestry*
Weaver Curriculum • 714-688-3126
Konos Character Curriculum • 214-669-8337
Alta Vista Curriculum • 800-544-1397
Tapestry • 800-705-7487
Unit Study: *Multi-Level Teaching is For You!* mini and audio by Joyce Herzog • 800-745-8212

Mrs. Average Homeschooler already has enough materials for the next four years if she goes at it full-time and never rests. She would do well to choose one or two skills per child to emphasize and reevaluate every six months. She would also be blessed by having someone to be accountable to. This would best be someone who can say, "Yes, darling, you have done enough. Your children are fine. I'm so proud of you!" As to curriculum, look over the shoulder of Mrs. Hopeful and drool. If you haven't tried any of those, go ahead and look, but be very careful about buying!

Mrs. Troubled Young Homeschooler will find it difficult to find anything that satisfies. She is likely to purchase many more materials than she can use, always looking for the one curriculum that will "fix" her homeschool. The tactic which would best suit her would be to designate one hour each day to concentrate on her school-age child. She could split that hour between reading and math and hope to catch a few minutes at another time to read aloud to both children. One of the "yearbooks" (fat workbook covering a whole grade and available from most homeschool suppliers) might be helpful to help her stay on track without much preparation or work. As her toddler grows and Origami learns to read and write, perhaps she will find it easier to cope with her situation. Learning games may help her now. They will make it more fun for her and her child and make her learning time more effective. It is important for her and her child that she "keep it simple" for if she is overwhelmed, she will simply quit. Something for reading and math and some games to cover the rest should be plenty for now.
The following material would be plenty for Mrs. Troubled:
F.L.A.G.S. 704-684-0429
Scaredy Cat Reading System by Joyce Herzog • 800-745-8212
School in a Box by Joyce Herzog • 800-745-8212
Math: store-bought workbooks like *Basic Skills Practice*, *Golden Step Up Series,* or *Kindergarten Yearbook*

Mrs. Terrific First Year Homeschooler will want materials that are fun for her and her child. She may change from time to time to keep herself and her child interested and stimulated. Because of her commitment and creativity, she will adapt and delight in whatever she chooses, so she won't be as hard to please as others might be.
Mrs. Terrific needs to check out the following:
Math: *MathUSee, Making Math Meaningful, Moving with Mathmatics*

Reading: *Scaredy Cat Reading* by Joyce Herzog • 800-745-8212
Five in a Row • 816-331-5769 • http://www.fiveinarow.com
School in a Box by Joyce Herzog • 800-745-8212
Dinah Zike's (**DinahMight Activities**) books beginning with *Big Book of Books and Activities*

Mrs. Houseful Homeschooler has her hands full, but considers idleness the devil's playground and is usually content. She will need materials for the older ones that are pretty much done independently. The older ones will help teach the younger ones and could be blessed by materials that are easy for them to understand and apply. The younger ones will learn much by the wonderful atmosphere and learning tools in their environment.
Five in a Row • 816-331-5769 • http://www.fiveinarow.com
Hands On and Beyond • 607-722-6563
Scaredy Cat Reading System and *School in a Box* by Joyce Herzog • 800-745-8212
Middle School and Up: *Trisms, Far Above Rubies, Plants Grown Up, Polished Cornerstones*
Sport Time • 800-477-5075
Refer to special needs companies such as **DLM, ARC, Attainment Company, Conover Company, Jesana Ltd., Laureate, Lekotex, My Clothes are Super, ProEd, Steck Vaughn, Therapro, Therapy Skill Builders, Woodbine House**, and so on. See General Resource Section.

Mrs. "I Don't Know what to do with Johnny" Homeschooler will need to concentrate on one difficulty at a time and try to discover and encourage the gifts and talents as well. Meanwhile, she must give him alternative ways of learning and expressing the information he knows. If the child does not read, he must be given every possible opportunity to learn through other avenues until he masters that skill. If he does not write, he must be given opportunities to show, do, point, tell, or make. If he is not a good listener, she will have to show him and cheerfully and patiently repeat the same idea a million times.
Reading: *Scaredy Cat Reading System* or *Writing Road to Reading*
Writing: *Understanding Writing* or *Writing Strands*
Math: *MathUSee, Mastering Mathmatics, Lockblock Logic, "Key to" Series, Basic College Mathematics Series*

Chapter Four

Education Styles

There are different ways to think about education. You will choose the style of education of your family as you determine how to homeschool and what materials to use. It is best to make an informed decision **before** you begin. Think about planning a long vacation. You haven't discussed or decided where you are going. You don't have a map. You will be gone six weeks and the whole family is going. You begin to pack the car with the "normal" vacation needs and head out. You find yourself meandering north from Denver in September. Before long, you begin to wish you'd brought heavy winter clothing and climbing gear. Uncomfortably cold, you decide to turn southeast and hit the highways for Florida. Once you get there, you find it necessary to invest in a wardrobe of summer clothes and swimming attire. "If only" you'd known where you were going, you could have saved time and money. "If only" you'd planned, you could have enjoyed the sites and chosen the route that most fit your preferences.

None of us would neglect to plan for a vacation, but many of us begin the journey into homeschool with no planning and no goal in mind. We pull the kids out of school and then begin to ask, "What curriculum should I buy?" Problem is, no one can answer that question unless they know you, your children, and what type of education you prefer. It would be far better if you answer some important questions first. The following material is quoted with permission from a brochure called *"Choosing Curriculum That's Right For You"* written by Susan Simpson of **Common Sense Press.**

There are three questions you must ask.
1. What is education?
2. What are the roles of the teacher and the student?
3. What is the role of the curriculum?

The Classroom Approach

The most common approach used by teachers with a classroom of 25-30 students. Many homeschoolers also use this approach.

What is education?
In this approach, the student takes in information, usually through a textbook or lecture. The student then gives the information back to the teacher through a project or test. Often, the textbooks will teach the same material year after year, adding a bit of new information each year. For example, American History may be taught for six consecutive years, adding new information each year.

What are the roles of teacher and student?
This approach sees the student as a learner who is able to take in bits and pieces of information, and put them together to form the big picture. Short term retention, via making a good test score, is stressed and rewarded. The teacher's main job is to follow the curriculum. These teachers believe that the curriculum creators know more about the students than the teacher does. If the student has difficulty, most proponents of this approach will recommend that the teacher force the student to conform to the curriculum. In that sense, it is a "one size fits all" approach.

What is the role of the curriculum?
In the Classroom Approach, curriculum is the most important part of education.

Pros & Cons of The Classroom Approach
- Possible high standardized test scores in early years
- Teacher has little input in curriculum
- Students may simply master the tests, rather than the material
- Students often become bored
- Students who do not fit the curriculum will feel inferior
- Students learn "factoids" rather than the big picture

The Life Approach
Also known as "Unschooling" or "Relaxed homeschooling", those who travel this route believe that education takes place primarily through life itself.

What is education?
In this approach, education is accomplished by developing a student's interests. Proponents of this approach believe that the skills of life will be learned as the student develops and grows, being allowed to discover life at his or her own pace. Often, this education includes a business or service project. Specific skills are not usually targeted, but will be focused upon as needed.

What are the roles of teacher and student?
The student is seen as a naturally curious learner who will learn in the proper environment. The teacher is primarily a resource to the student. The teacher's main job is to create an atmosphere of learning and to be a learner as well. The belief is that the student will model the teacher's life as an effective learner, thus the student will become an effective learner. Beyond that, it is somewhat difficult to define the teacher's role, because every teacher is so different in this approach.

What is the role of the curriculum?
There is no curriculum in The Life Approach. If curriculum is used, it is for reading or math only.

Pros and Cons of The Life Approach
- Students are aware of interests and abilities
- Students develop thinking skills and become independent thinkers

- Little pressure on teachers
- Possible low standardized test scores in early years
- Opinions vary as to whether or not students will learn all they need

The Applied Approach

In this approach, "Application" is the emphasis in education.

What is education?

This approach emphasizes the application of knowledge. A student who can complete a math sheet on subtracting money should also be able to make change in the store. Of course not all information is so readily applied to life. This is overcome by actually doing the things being taught or by finding a context in the student's life for the new information. The age, development, and "readiness" of the student is always kept in mind. Reading may be taught in 1st grade or 3rd grade depending on the child, for example.

What are the roles of teacher and student?

The student is an individual to be treated in an age appropriate manner. It is believed that a student will better learn a new concept if he or she is walked through it and then allowed to do it or apply it, rather than just being told about it. The teacher's role is very important because the teaching parent knows the student better than anyone else. This approach gives the teacher the power to discern where students need help and how to give it to them.

What is the role of curriculum?

Curriculum is seen as a means to an end, not as the end itself. It is used in a manner that is best for the student. Actual curriculum choices can make the teacher's job easier or harder. An age appropriate, flexible program is best.

Pros & Cons of The Applied Approach

- Students' individual needs are met
- Student gains confidence, not being compared with others
- Better and longer retention
- Education becomes a practical part of life
- Possible low standardized test scores in early years

Let's Study Ducks!

Let's look at the study of "Ducks" from each approach we have just examined.

The Classroom Approach

The study will begin because it is the next chapter in the science book. The student will read the section about ducks in the textbook, answer the questions at the end of the chapter, and perhaps create a project on ducks. The teacher will give the student a test to complete, which will determine if the student remembers certain facts about ducks. It is probable that the student will never see an actual duck.

The Life Approach
The study will begin because the teacher or the student has an interest in ducks. The student and teacher may go to the library to find books on ducks, build a pond, hatch eggs, and even raise ducks for food or to sell. The student will read for comprehension as he or she learns what ducks need to survive. The student will write and think in order to create a schedule for feeding the ducks and cleaning after them. There will be education in math (food cost calculations), science (hatching of eggs), social sciences (the need for ducks in our world), and much more.

The Application Approach
The study of ducks may begin because the teacher has decided that it is time to learn about ducks, whether the child has expressed interest in them or not. The teacher will find books on ducks and maybe a read-aloud novel that includes a duck character. A published curriculum on ducks may be used. The teacher will present certain facts about ducks that she determines are important. Age-appropriate activities will be included to reinforce this information. The family may visit a duck pond and then write Grandma a letter about the trip. The student will be working on math and language arts or reading while this study is taking place. These subjects may or may not have anything to do with ducks.

(Back to Joyce) You may choose one education style in math and another in the other subjects. You may choose one style for one child and a different style for another. You may combine styles and approaches. Most of us, by default, pattern our homeschool after the education we experienced. This can be counterproductive. Whether you are just beginning or in your 8th year of homeschooling, it is never too late or too early to look at your goals and plans. Consider and meditate on the following two dictionary definitions of education. Search the Scriptures for relevant commands, exhortations or examples. Consider the example of Jesus as He taught His disciples and the multitudes. Consider why you have decided to homeschool. Try to answer the three questions above for yourself: **What is education? What are the roles of the teacher and the student? What is the role of the curriculum?** Then choose the materials which best meet the needs you have identified.

1828 Webster's
EDUCA'TION, n. [L. educatio.] The bringing up, as of a child, instruction; formation of manners. Education comprehends all that series of instruction and discipline which is intended to **enlighten the understanding, correct the temper, and form the manners and habits of youth,** and fit them for usefulness in their future stations. To give children a good education in manners, arts and science, is important; to give them a religious education is indispensable; and an immense responsibility rests on parents and guardians who neglect these duties.

American Heritage Dictionary
1. The act or process of educating or being educated.
2. The knowledge or skill obtained or developed by a learning process.
3. A program of instruction of a specified kind or level.
4. The field of study that is concerned with the pedagogy of teaching and learning.
5. An instructive or enlightening experience.

Chapter Five

What Grade Level?

What is a grade level? Think about these questions:

     Is "third grade" the third year of every child's education?

     Is every "third grader" doing "third grade" work?

     Is every "third grade" in the country teaching the same level of skills?

The answer to every question is, "NO!"

What is a grade level? It is an arbitrary designation which, historically, is about 150 years old and was initially invented to help group children for learning in an institutional setting. There are no "grade levels" in the Bible or in history before late 1700's when people began to bring children together to be educated in large groups. Still, if we could have some agreement as to what they mean, they might be of help for us to describe where a child is on the learning scale.

At one point in history, all new students started with the "Primer." When they finished that (whether it took months or years) they went on to the Second Book. That is a logical system with merit. The system we have now defies logic. Stop thinking, "He's five; he's in kindergarten. He must master these (X, Y, Z) skills. Begin to think more like: "These are kindergarten skills. When he's mastered these skills, he's finished kindergarten." And remember: he may be in different grade levels in different subjects because children do not always progress evenly in all subjects. Know also that grade level expectations differ considerably from one curriculum to another. Some curriculum developers seem to think that children learn everything in kindergarten and review for the next six years.

The best thing (especially in reading and math) is to give each child a placement test for the curricula you choose to use (if they have one). At other times, too, it is helpful to have a broad knowledge of what grade level your child is working at, how to gauge a simple book they want to read or a piece they write. The following list is suggestive only. It is approximate and not cast in concrete. It will not fit with every program on the market. It is based on my many years of teaching in the public schools in the 70's and 80's. It may already be watered down from a generation before, but truthfully, I think it is more realistic than many of those approaches that abound today which cram it all down in the first year or two and then review. Realize that many children will be ahead of this and do both Kindergarten and First Grade before they are six. Fine, that is no problem. Others may struggle with Kindergarten reading/spelling when they are eight and doing 3rd grade math. That, too, is no problem – unless you make it one! This is only to give you a very broad idea of traditional grade level expectations so you know what level of books/workbooks to purchase to match your child's level of progress.

Kindergarten

Reading/Spelling: Letter names (and/or sounds), perhaps some short vowel words
Writing: Traces and copies letters of the alphabet, may also write the alphabet and copy words
Math: Counts orally to 30 (perhaps 100); writes numerals and counts objects to 10 (perhaps 20); adds to 5 (perhaps 10)

First Grade

Reading/Spelling: One syllable words, especially short vowel words (like cat, run, hop, fix, and red); simple sentences (like I can run. He sat up. The cat can jump.); possibly silent E words.
Writing: Writes words and simple sentences
Math: Reads and writes numbers to 100, addition facts, possibly some simple subtraction

Second Grade

Reading/Spelling: Short and long vowels; some r-controlled (like hard, her, and turn) and aw/au (like paw, haul); two and three syllable words. Slightly more complex sentence structure (like The children ran to the open van. Mother and Father are fixing supper at the campsite.)
Writing: Writes simple sentences (up to 8 words) and simple stories (2 to 5 sentences)
Math: Reads and writes numbers to 1000, addition and subtraction facts, carrying in addition

Third Grade

Reading/Spelling: Gains accuracy with most phonetic words and a large sight vocabulary; begins to read chapter books and reads for enjoyment
Writing: Expands simple story writing; introduced to concept of paragraph and friendly letter; writes simple experience (first person) narration and very simple book report
Math: Reads and writes numbers to 10,000; addition and subtraction with and without renaming and in columns; begins multiplication

Fourth Grade

Reading/Spelling: Reads chapter books with understanding; begins critical thinking in reading; learns practical spelling words
Writing: Develops previous skills; introduced to business letter, simple first person narrative, simple fictional story, book report and very simple encyclopedia report
Math: Masters counting, addition, subtraction and multiplication, introduced to division and fractions

Fifth Grade

Reading/Spelling: Competent readers and spellers
Writing: Continues developing above, introduced to encyclopedia report and poetry
Math: Masters division, fractions and decimals; introduced to percents and geometry

Sixth Grade

Reading/Spelling: Competent readers and spellers
Writing: Writes paragraphs, stories and reports, including research report using several sources
Math: Masters addition, subtraction, multiplication and division of any amount; competent with fractions, decimals, percentages, and geometry with all 2 and 3-dimensional shapes

Chapter Six

Getting Back to Basics

We constantly hear hype about getting "back to basics," but I don't think many of us know what that means. Let's explore for a moment what is historically and Biblically the basis of education.

Historically, children have been in the homes for their youngest years – usually through age 7. At some times in our history, those young ones were taught some basic understanding of counting and calculations and to read – or at least the alphabet. What has been consistent until the past century or so, is that those young ones were taught still more basic things. Those cradle and toddler years were the years when emotional security, spiritual depth, and beginning work skills were the focus of life. We seem to have thrown away the wisdom of the ages to concentrate, instead, on early academics. I believe in early learning. I believe that all children are learning from birth – and learning is to be encouraged at all ages. I don't believe, however, that there is great virtue in a child learning to read at a very young age. In fact, I know several families who have regretted that their very young children could **and did** read whatever they could see.

We are creating problems with our children in our "new society." We start them young, filling their heads with knowledge, giving them freedom to choose their own behavior, serving them and picking up after them. Then they grow smart-mouthed and arrogant and we wonder what happened.

Little children want to follow us around. They want to do whatever we are doing. They want to "help." We see them as a nuisance and tell them to "go and play." We let them be their own boss as long as they are not endangering themselves or others. Later, when they are 5 or 6, we call them to ourselves, try to take authority over them, and try to make them want to listen to us teach them. Then, when they are 8 to 10, we try to get them interested in working and helping. They are no longer interested! They have been the successful boss of their waking hours and are not interested in voluntarily giving that authority over to a person who has consistently told them to "go away." Read Jeremiah 2:30 to see what God thinks about this. "In vain have I smitten your children; they received no correction." In other words: "Because you did not train and correct your children and train them in obedience, I can call until My voice is hoarse and they don't listen or respond because they are not accustomed to listening or obeying." Remediating **that** is far more important than "teaching" early academics!

Solution: Include little ones in your "real life work" whenever possible. Encourage their interest, their attempts, and their willingness to work and help. Mold their character. Fill their heads with Scripture. Cuddle and nurture them. Keep them with you and keep them busy. They will be developing physical and social skills needed for life as they grow under your watchful eye. If there's time, some academics are fine, but they should NOT be the emphasis at this age, and they should be within the context of real life, counting the forks at the table, singing the alphabet song, and so on. Encourage them to help with the daily work. Little ones can set the table, sort clothes, fold washcloths, slice bananas, put things in the garbage, pull up a comforter on a bed, and so on.

What is basic in the early years (under five):
> Training them to obey
> Teaching them to listen and respond quickly the first time they are called
> Building into them the work habit
> Helping them to memorize Scripture
> Showing them to (and how to) look to God for solutions
> Giving them plenty of opportunity to be servants to others
> Teaching them to cheerfully live under authority

Around five to seven (some younger, some older), many will show interest in reading and writing and numbers; **wait for their cues**. When your child can recognize fine differences between styles of silverware, sort and match similar items of clothing, toys or screws/nails, etc., name a variety of flowers, birds, or trees, and consistently remember the names of many friends and family members, he is probably ready to begin reading instruction. When he can draw the simple shapes, trace pictures, and cut out circles and squares, he is ready to learn to print. When he can recite the numbers from 1 to 5, have him begin counting objects: the buttons on his shirt, the people in the room, glasses at the table, etc. If you wait for this type of clues, your instruction time is likely to be smoother and more effective. We can start younger, work harder, and take longer, or wait until they are ready and soar through.

The primary grades (K-3) are primarily for developing the skills of reading (letters, words, sentences, and stories), writing (letters, words, sentences, and factual, experience-related stories), and arithmetic (count, add, subtract).

The upper elementary years (grades 4-6) are for polishing and extending those skills: reading for information, pleasure, developing critical reading skills; taking arithmetic on to multiplication, division, fractions and decimals; writing reports, beginning research skills, expanding knowledge of basic history, science, and geography, broadening experience with styles of literature.

Junior high sees the extension and refinement of all fore-mentioned skills, beginnings of discussion, debate, and exploration of a broad base of skills and knowledge.

High School is the time to polish skills, explore some topics in depth and begin to specialize in the child's interests.

Chapter Seven

What Can They Do By Themselves?

Many of us are frustrated because we have to be with every child all the time. That is impossible even if we have only one child! Yet when we leave them to work alone, they fritter their time, get distracted, do a sloppy job, leave, or in other ways avoid working. Some of that comes with maturity, but there are almost always things every child can do independently at least for a short time. Here are some ideas to get you started. Ages are approximate; children differ tremendously.

Independent Tasks

Age	Skill	Topic
2-4 years	Copy design with blocks Sort Match Build Dress (self or doll) Do simple puzzle Water Play (small container) Pour (sand, salt, rice) Fill Put in Sequence (large to small, small to large, one to five, etc.)	Colors Shapes Sizes Sequence Numbers Alphabet
5-7 years	All of Above (more complex) plus: Color Copy Trace Draw Write Build Cut and Paste Make Count	All of Above (more complex) plus: Reading Math

Independent Tasks, Continued

Age	Skill	Topic
7-9	All of Above (more complex) plus: Read Dinah Zike's Activities Computer	All of Above (more complex) plus: Alphabetical Order Spelling Science History
9-12	All of Above (more complex) plus: Photo Album Letter Writing Correct Keyboard Skills Practice Instrument Nurture (pets, children, senior citizens)	All of Above (more complex) plus: Geography Literature Music Art Literature
12-15	All of Above (more complex) plus: Record Information Projects Reports Keep Records Volunteer Apprentice Childcare Teach Younger Ones	All of Above (in greater depth) plus: Individual Interests and Hobbies

Chapter Eight

Start Your Year Out Right!

- Know where you are going and what you will use to get there. What is your goal?
    Possibilities:
        Teach 3 R's: reading, writing, and arithmetic
        Encourage 4 R's: Reasoning, Relationships, Responsibility and Remembering
        Cover a stated curriculum (and thereby make your children meet someone else's
            goals)
        "Catch up" to grade level
        Develop skills needed for life
        Master basic skills (name them)
        Introduce all subjects according to some expert's schedule
        Teach skills your child is ready for
        Expose your child to all kinds of information
        Soak your child in God's Word and His Ways
        Follow your child's inclinations in learning and mastering skills
        Explore learning with your child
        Train your child in the way *he* should go
        Provide many learning opportunities
        Give your child many experiences with different people, ideas, skills, and media
        Teach them to decide
        Teach them to observe, appreciate, serve

- Get excited! Have something new and exciting planned so that you are enthused.

- Buy paper, folders, and other supplies for the year **in late July or early August** (before-school
    sales)! They won't be cheaper.

- Read aloud to your child until he is old enough to read aloud to his children.
    Always have an on-going novel, biography, or series that you read when you can.

- Teach your child the five finger rule.
    When selecting a book, he puts down one finger for each word he can't read.
    If five fingers are down on one page, the book is too hard, select a different one.

- Enjoy your child and spend time with him.

- Be ready to take advantage of "teachable moments" when he asks a question or shows an
    interest.

• Be ready to take a break when you or they need it.

• Have something in mind that each can do independently.

• Use common 3"x5" file boxes with dividers and index cards to teach skills and organization.
> Letters A-Z
>> Match same letters (example: all capital A's of different print fonts)
>> Match upper/lower case
>> Match letter to beginning sound pictures
>> Spell: Bring me a blank card for the beginning sound. Write the first three letters of the word you are thinking of. Look it up. Write it on card. Bring it back for me to check. Draw a picture of it beside the word.

> Numerals
>> Match numerals
>> Match numeral with number of dots or object
>> Match numeral with word
>> Match numeral with problems which share that answer
>>> For Multiplication facts this will automatically teach factors!

• Keep a journal. Include the following:
Weekly through the year, choose a paper from each subject area to keep in a notebook. Keep a prayer request list with answers. List all books read (whether read to the child or independently doesn't matter, but each book counts only once.)

• Stay energized.
Throughout the year, when things bog down, find something new and exciting to get new life into your school.

• Education includes many learning opportunities!
Don't be afraid to count cooking, learning to tell time, or measuring as math, read-aloud as reading, and writing a letter to grandma or a sick friend as language arts!

Chapter Nine

Take A Snapshot of Your Child's Progress!

Here is an easy way to evaluate and record where your child is in maturity, reading, spelling, language, and math informally and without the stress of testing. Add this to the portfolio you are keeping to show his progress. This portfolio should include samples of his work every month, special reports or pictures of projects and special activities, a list of prayers and their answers, books read (even if read aloud to him), field trips, and personal skills (like learned to ride a bike, or mastered swimming the side-stroke).

As I am revising and updating this book, a story from this season's travel comes to mind. One mom asked if she could show me what her child had done. I readily agreed. She brought the results of doing the following assignment five different times, two months apart. This was her child's first year of school and her first year to homeschool. The child had progressed from not knowing the alphabet or being able to write any words to writing the alphabet, many words and simple sentences. Mom also reported that she was now reading simple books and interested in learning. We were impressed and pleased with her progress and the mom was obviously proud to show her child's accomplishments. Then she told me "the rest of the story." After finishing this, she had to put her child through the "hard testing" according to her state's law. Her child's achievement test scores had just come in. She showed me the results. It recorded two months progress in reading. Mom shared her thoughts. "If I'd only had the achievement test, I'd have been devastated. We worked so hard. If I really thought my daughter had made only two months progress in all that time, I'd have given up and sent her back to school. I'd have concluded that I wasn't fit to teach and she wasn't learning anything. But having this concrete record of her progress made all the difference in the world. I now understand that the achievement test just wasn't asking the questions that fit what we'd done. Now I'm ready to continue and know that we're making progress."

We all need to see progress or we won't keep working. This simple activity will show you **and** your students how much they've learned. The sentences reflect their spelling, writing, and thinking abilities as well as their vocabulary and mental maturity. The math problems reflect what they are currently able to do independently. Their handwriting shows immediately their maturity and skill with a pencil. So much for so little effort! Please – take the time to do this at least twice a year!

Parent Instructions: Over a period of days (as many as necessary to comfortably finish) have your child complete the following assignment. As he works, keep a separate sheet of notes giving specific information on your observations. Do not allow him to consult any references such as a copy of the alphabet, a calendar, or a dictionary. Encourage him to draw a single line through errors rather than erasing so you can see any areas of insecurity. Do not specify printing or cursive or give reminders. If he seeks specific instructions (What letter comes next? or How do you spell _____?), encourage him to do what he thinks is best, but assure him that you would rather see a sample of **his** best work even if it includes errors than a sample of *your own* work!

Student Assignment

1) Name and date your paper.

2) Draw a man.

3) Write the alphabet. (If he only does **either** capitals **or** lower case, when he finishes, have him do the other. If his is a combination of both, go on to the number four.)

4) List 10 of the hardest words you are quite sure you can spell correctly. (He should think of these words by himself and not be coached.)

5) Write 5 sentences (3 if that would be quite a struggle).

6) Writing Skills: Have student do one of the following assignments. Choose the one which is challenging, but not impossible.
    a) Write a story of several paragraphs
    b) Write one paragraph.
    c) Discuss a simple topic he knows something about such as dogs or baseball or brothers and write 5 sentences about that topic

7) Write down one sample problem for each operation (addition, subtraction, multiplication, and division, also fractions and decimals if he is to that level) that will give you an idea of his level of mastery. Have him work the problems, then mark them correct or incorrect, but do not ask him to make corrections. You need to see his work and thought process.

Take an actual photograph of your child as he works. Attach it to this work.

As he works through the assignment, take your own notes in the following manner:
Make note of amount of time required for each portion of the assignment (Name and date paper, three minutes, etc.). Note any specific helpful information. (Sample: Needed to sing the alphabet to remember letters after H. Repeated singing the entire alphabet seven times to finish.)

Chapter Ten
Infant & Early Childhood Education

If you are dealing with a young or profoundly handicapped child, there are materials for you! If your child is blind or deaf, contact the organizations listed in the Special Education Resource Lists (pages 101 and 103), HSLDA, and NATHHAN. They have some helpful information on parenting children with these specific problems.

Remember, though, that even a handicapped child is first of all a child. A sleeping problem is a sleeping problem whether your child is "normal" or handicapped. The same is true with a discipline problem or inattention. I have seen two opposite tendencies in schools that work with special needs children. One looks at them as "poor little children" who should always be happy and never be stressed or pushed. The other says these children should sit all day with a book in their hands and "read" and "write" even if they have no verbal (let alone written) language. Both are extreme and to be avoided at all costs. Handicapped children are children first. They will have all the normal growing up problems and a few extra ones. Like all children, if they are undisciplined at age two, they will be obnoxious at age five and fifteen.

If you have a special needs child, he needs loving, disciplined structure even more than other children. He can learn, but he needs limits and opportunities just like any other child. Encourage him early to try, to explore, to believe he can do things until he proves otherwise. But just as important, do not allow him to control you any more than you would any other child! He is a child! You are the adult! Remember who is in control!

Whether your child is "normal" or "special," here are some good materials to consider.

Slow and Steady Get Me Ready: A Parents' Handbook, Oberlander
Bio-Alpha, Inc. • P.O. Box 7190 • Fairfax Station, VA 22039-7190
This treasure gives one activity per week for the first five years of life! It lets you know what skills are appropriate for each developmental age, and gives appropriate activities to guide the development of the skills. A video supplement and a checklist are also available.

In Time and With Love: Caring for the Special Needs Baby, Segal
This little book gives special information for parenting a young special needs child. It has black and white photos to enable you to see the activities in action.

evelopmentally Disabled Children: The ME Book, Lovaas (Pro-Ed)
gives how-to information for the profoundly or severely handicapped young child. It
ep by step learning of very basic skills from obeying simple commands, increasing
vocalizations, toileting skills, dressing, and on to more advanced things like stopping echolalia
(mindlessly repeating sounds and words) and psychotic talk (disassociated conversation),
teaching phrases and sentences, and building time concepts. Combined with much love and a
gentle spirit, this method has much to offer.

Train Up A Child, Michael and Debi Pearl
1010 Pearl Road • Pleasantville, TN 37147
Too many of us have attempted to make discipline alone substitute for training and discipline.
The Bible tells us to "train up a child in the way he should go." This is impossible unless we
understand what it means to train a child and have some good idea of how to accomplish it. This
book will make you laugh and cry – and teach you how to train your child!

Five in a Row
14901 Pineview Dr • Grandview, MO 64030-4509 • 816-331-5769
http://www.fiveinarow.com
Preschool and elementary curriculum based on reading a picture book five days in a row and
jumping from there into activities in language arts, math, history, geography, etc.

Picture Book Preschool by Sherry Diane Early
15707 Rill Lane • Houston, TX 77062 •
email: Stearly@earthlink.net
Similar to *Five in a Row,* but much less involved. A list of 7 books on one topic with some
suggested activities for each week of the preschool or kindergarten year

Chapter Eleven

Bible, Spiritual, Religious, & Character Training

I can't emphasize enough the importance of teaching moral and spiritual values at an early age. We tend to get the cart before the horse when we start early academics and ignore spiritual and character training. The Bible says, "Knowledge puffs up," and a head full of learning without moral values does just that. Before age five (and up to seven for many children) there is nothing more important than teaching **and** modeling pure spiritual values. Remember, values are caught more than taught, so watch your step!

Stepping Stones to Bigger Faith for Little People, Joyce Herzog
Forty devotions written at a second grade reading level teach profound truths of Scripture for young (in age or mentality) children and families. Audio version has the author reading aloud the print and children singing the Bible verses set to original music. Sequel *Stepping Stones to Praise and Worship* (written at a slightly higher reading level) is also available.

Bible Study Guide for All Ages, Dr. Donald and Mary Baker
P.O. Box 2608 •-Russellville, AR 72811 • 501-967-0577 • FAX 501-890-6262
800-745-8212 • EMAIL: tjudd@cei.net
A series of four units (about $30 each) to teach the Bible to families and other multi-age groups. Four units cover many Bible characters (not introduced in chronological order). Each unit is divided into 104 lessons and includes drills, review plan, scripture, vocabulary explanations, questions to ask, map work, a time line, songs and an easy-to-draw (stick figures) visual idea. Some of the lessons in Unit One also have colorful worksheets available for non-readers, low readers, or regular readers, which could stand alone.

Book of Remembrance
Eternal Foundations Curriculum • P.O. Box 1213 • Atascadero, CA 93423
805-466-1910
You can create your own family Bible notebooks with these age-integrated, reproducible Bible reading response, character development, spiritual journal and prayer and praise worksheets. A great boon to those who want a simple form to use in those topics.

Character First
Character First! Education • 520 W. Main Street • Oklahoma City, OK 73102 • 405-815-0001, ext. 150 • FAX 405-235-5826

Character First, continued:
This series of booklets, character cards, posters, audio tapes, and training videos is excellent to teach and train character qualities through study of nature and history, coloring, collecting cards, songs, and doing activities. These are basically secular so they can be used in public school and other non-religious settings, but are based upon sound Biblical principles and correlate well with the following *Character Sketches* .

Character Sketches
Institute in Basic Life Principles • Oak Brook, IL
These three volumes are wonderful for looking at various character qualities through nature, Scripture and history. Accompanying coloring books and card game are also useful. Especially good, I think, if Dad leads this and Mom accompanies it with the *Character First* activities.

Family Discipleship Manual
Eternal Foundations Curriculum • P.O. Box 1213 • Atascadero, CA 93423 • 805-466-1910
This book will enable you to lead your whole family in a deep study of the three basic teachings: the Word, prayer, and Christian service even if you yourself are a beginner in Bible knowledge. It is thorough, well-written and helps get your children into the Word: reading, understanding and highlighting in colors according to topic. It includes 100 lessons and activity pages as well as project suggestions for each of the three units. This book uses simple object lessons, provides different activities for all ages and deals with tough issues like persecution of Christians, spiritual warfare, and other religions and their beliefs.

Listen, Color, & Learn: **Four Volumes**
These books allow young energetic children to color as you read and discuss the Psalms.

Hands-On Character Building, by Rick and Marilyn Boyer
This is an incredible book of projects which instill godly character. Some can be done in moments, others take weeks. Most can be adapted for many ages and abilities.

Big Book of Books and Activities: **Old Testament** or **New Testament**, by Dinah Zike
This series is filled with everything you need to make vivid three-dimensional visuals with your children. Doing these activities will get them involved and increase their understanding and retention.

How to Have Kids With Character: **Even If Your Kids Are Characters** by Brown
Activities (designated 1-7 years or 8-15 years), Scriptures, slogans and crafts to develop twelve character traits in your children. Consider your child's maturity age, not his chronological age.

What the Bible is All About for Young Explorers by Blankenbaker
This treasure helps children from third grade up really understand the Bible! It includes illustrated timelines, information about life, color photographs of the Holy Land, summaries of every chapter of the Bible, maps, archeological information, outlines and more. A wonderful resource for 8-adult understanding of scriptures and what it means.

Chapter Twelve
Points to Consider When Choosing A Math Curriculum

Early math includes the same basic skill sequence whether the child is gifted, normal, or special needs. The main difference is in the manner of presentation, the age of readiness, and the amount of practice needed for mastery. Many of the early skills can be taught without special materials or books. Start at home with real things around you.

Teach your child to:

Count to five, ten, then twenty
One to one correspondence (Count objects one by one)
Numeral recognition (Name numerals 1-10)
Match numeral to correct number of objects
Join sets (groups of objects) and answer "How many now?"

Methods Sequence:

1. Math around the house: (How many hands do you have? How many eyes, fingers, toes, etc.? How many people in the family? How many forks will we need for supper? Dad is not here tonight, how many places should we set? and so on.)

2. Much use of a variety of manipulatives (rods, small toys, buttons etc.) in the following activities:

       a. counting one by one
       b. joining sets to 5, then 10
       c. taking away a given number
       d. matching number of teddy bears and circles, etc.
       e. sorting by color, shape, size, etc.
       f. making sets of the same number (like three buttons each for Mom and me)

3. Follow this by using a hundred chart with activities

Writing numerals and number words can be taught with handwriting and spelling. For children whose writing skills are weaker than their computational skills, consider using moveable numerals such as magnetic letters, stamps of the numerals with a stamp pad, a typewriter, a computer, or letting them dictate to someone. For more detail on teaching K-3 math skills without workbooks, see Ruth Beechick's ***An Easy Start in Arithmetic*** (page 42). If any of your children have special needs, remember: special needs children don't always accomplish skills in the same amount of time, but usually do progress in the same sequence as other learners. Paper and pencil and book activities aren't really needed until the very basic concepts are mastered.

Sometime after grade three skills are reached, you might consider spending a year using some supplemental worksheets such as ***Essential Learning Workbooks***, plus ***Grocery Cart Math.*** By mental age ten to twelve, work with real math again in terms of budgeting, keeping track of a savings account or checking account, and assisting with shopping. Don't feel that you have to follow a single curriculum and stick with it for every grade level. If you prefer a single curriculum, check out ***MathUSee, Moving With Math, Touch Math, Mastering Mathematics,*** or ***Miquon Math***. The important thing is that your child learn to understand math concepts and manipulate numbers adequately to survive in society to whatever degree he is able.

There are two basic approaches to math: **the spiral curriculum** and **the sequential curriculum.** The spiral curriculum introduces many topics quite quickly, reviews them frequently, and repeats them from year to year. This is the type of curriculum used in traditional texts. The purpose is really classroom related. The theory is that some will catch it the first time around, some will need a second pass, and others will have to have it presented several times before they grasp it. For a very bright child, this becomes very boring. For a child who cannot do the mental gymnastics to continually change thinking patterns, this becomes very frustrating. The sequential curriculum presents material in a logical building sequence and assumes that once it is mastered, review is automatic as you build skill upon skill. That method alone may not provide enough practice for some learners. ***Moving With Math*** seems to do the best job of combining the two methods.

Everyone asks, "What is your favorite math program?" I don't have a favorite for several reasons. There are quite a few good ones. None of them will work for every child - or every family - or even for every year! Each one has drawbacks along with its assets. Some would be wonderful for a year or two, but drudgery for the long haul. Don't expect me to make this decision for you. You will have to invest time and effort into looking at each program and comparing its advantages and disadvantages with your family's needs.

Math Skill Inventory, by Letz Farmer
Mastery Publications • 90 Hillside Lane • Arden, NC 287-4-9709• 704-684-0429
http://www.masterypublications.com • masterypub@aol.com
This deserves to stand alone as a very helpful tool for every homeschool. It is a test you can administer to determine what math skills your child has mastered and which need to be addressed. This test can be used alone or compliments Mastering Mathematics curriculum by the same author. Administer the test, grade the answers, transfer checkmarks to a "Skills at a Glance" page and you'll see just what your child still needs to learn! Then you can plug him into any curriculum and decide which pages he may skip because he's already mastered the skills.

Chapter Thirteen

Comparison of Math Programs

Key considerations in math programs include:
   adequate space for a child with motor problems to calculate and write an answer
   sequence of skills
   concrete presentation of concepts (manipulatives)
   relevance of story problems
   adequate amount of practice for children who need a great deal of repetition
   flexibility of pace

Traditional math programs (which require the copying of problems) are not usually a good choice for children with learning problems. They often miscopy and/or spend their entire math class copying and don't have time to work the problems! I've suggested to many moms if they want to use that type of curriculum and the child struggles to write and copy, that they (the moms) copy the page for the student. The moms always insist they don't want to spend the time hand-copying each problem because they have more important things to do. Perhaps there are more important things for your child to do as well. You will probably do well to choose a workbook approach and even then look to see whether there is enough room for your child to write the answer. If you choose a typical text, consider enlarging the pages mechanically (photo-copy at 125%) to make it easier to read and to give more space to work the problem and write in answers. If there is too much on a page for your child, try cutting the page into strips or sections. Reward the child for finishing one piece of the page and give him a break or a change of topics and try another part later in the day. It is all right to adapt material for your child.

Another thing to consider: **Calculator or not?** Well, in today's world we would be pretty lost without the use of a calculator. Children certainly need to be taught calculator skills. On the other hand we need to understand numbers and how to manipulate them. Perhaps a good compromise is using the calculator once a week or for correcting errors. For children who by age twelve or so continue to be unable to master basic operations in spite of plenty of learning opportunity and a variety of approaches, a calculator may be the answer.

With reluctant learners try to find a way to build in a reward for concentration and accuracy. With a sequential curriculum, try one of these approaches: If the first five problems are correctly solved, the rest of the page is skipped. If one in a row is missed, another row is required. If there are two or more errors, review the concept and finish the page. It is more difficult with a spiral curriculum. Have the child do only the even or odd problems. If they are correct, he may skip the others. Or try even problems (in lesson one) one day and odd problems (in lesson two) the next. Reward diligent accurate work if that is what you want to see in the future!

Comparison of Math Programs, Continued
An Easy Start in Arithmetic by Ruth Beechick
This is **the** way to start math as far as I'm concerned, as a natural outcome of events around the house. As these very basic concepts are mastered, consider any of the following materials.

Basic Skills Practice Workbooks
Essential Learning Products • P.O. Box 2607 • Columbus, OH 43216-2607
800-357-3570
The small size of the page and limited number of problems on a page make these a good choice for children with trouble concentrating for any length of time. They have workbooks to cover every area of math and are logically sequenced. The series on story problems is particularly good in that it emphasizes teaching a plan of action. If you are using manipulatives and allowing lots of exploration in a loosely-knit situation, but want to be sure you've covered the basics, this is the series for you! The small workbooks are non-intimidating for practice and give enough room for writing answers! Great supplement to manipulatives.

Developmental Mathematics by George Saad, Ph.D
Mathematics Programs Associates Inc. • P.O. Box 118 • Halesite, NY 11743
Small, incremental steps of learning with no glitz and an incredible amount of practice are the strength of this series of workbooks. They are compatible with any manipulatives, but do not incorporate any at all. Their biggest drawbacks as I see them are the tiny amount of space for writing answers, the concentration on writing, and the incredibly boring practice. The danger is that children figure out and follow the pattern to finish the page and don't internalize the concept at all. Some moms love this one and some kids hate it! (You can probably tell I'm with the kids!) One friend of mine becomes the "favorite mom" when she says, "You've got it! Congratulations! You don't have to do the next 3 pages."

Grocery Cart Math, by Jane Hansen
This excellent program will fill your older (11+) children with shopping savvy. A supplemental program, it is so intensive that it might best be the focus for a year while using some minimal workbook program or once a week along with a more structured program. Preparation is needed before going shopping with your children who will then need time to roam the store and make comparisons of prices, pounds, and other pertinent information. This will give structure to all those informal lessons our children need to learn before they are on their own!

Hands On Equations
Marvelous approach to hands on algebra which builds understanding. Uses concept of balance beam with blocks. Useful to enhance the self-esteem of younger learners ("I can do algebra!") or build understanding with older learners who "just can't get it."

Family Math
Games and activities to teach most math skills using real life situations and materials around the house. Great supplement for any math program!

Kaidy Educational Resources
P.O. Box 831853 • Richardson, TX 75083-1853
800-365-2439 • 972-234-6161 • FAX 800-425-2439 • FAX 972-234-5626
"Hands On Manipulatives are Universal Tools for Education!" I was delighted when I found this company. They have created products to enable students to see concepts and games to make math practice fun. This is NOT a math program, but its inexpensive components can be used to supplement whatever you are using. My favorite is *Basic Multi* which contains 9 cards and 9 small transparencies to create understanding and memorization of 81 times problems!

Key To... Workbooks
Key Curriculum Press • 2512 Martin Luther King Jr. Way • PO Box 2304 • Berkely, CA, 94702
Finally a source for special needs math at the junior high and high school level! These workbooks are clear, easy to read and understand, leave room for working and writing answers, and tackle the tough subjects like geometry, percent, fractions, decimals and even algebra! Lots of hands-on and fun paper activities to build geometry concepts. Write for a complete catalog, because they have more than I have room to tell you about!

Mad Minute
Not a full curriculum, these reproducible test sheets (minute with enough room to write answers!) for practice of math facts will beautifully supplement any program. Short intense practice builds concentration skills and time awareness along with math skills!

Making Math Meaningful by David Quine
Cornerstone Curriculum Project • 2006 Flat Creek • Richardson, TX, 75080
Detailed easy-to-understand instruction manuals direct the parents what to say in this one-on-one program which stresses mathematical reasoning through real life situations and manipulatives

Mastering Mathematics, Letz Farmer.
Mastery Publications • 90 Hillside Lane • Arden, NC 28704 • 704-684-0429
Designed for Christian homeschooling families with average, special needs, or bright students, this program has found success with special needs children. It is diagnostic (helps you determine what your child doesn't know), prescriptive (gives you what you need to teach missing skills), and systematic. It features optional presentations by grade levels or by topic (addition, multiplication, decimals, etc.). Work pages are clear and uncluttered and face a blank page for minimal visual distraction. Poster board manipulatives and games are included, but any rod system may be substituted nicely. The sequence is good, the instructions are clear, the pace is flexible, and the story problems are decidedly Christian. Clear, uncluttered pages have adequate space for answer. You may want to fill in with additional practice and story problems.

Math Made Meaningful
Alpha Plus • P.O. Box 185 • Chewsville, MD 21721
More than a math program, this is a math curriculum *service* dedicated to assisting you to find the best math resources and use them effectively. Math workshops are available. Academic services include planning, evaluation, individualized, and underlined achievement testing. Send $1 and your address for a copy of "Fear Not Math," which includes resources and workshop information.

Mathematics Their Way and ***Mathematics...A Way of Thinking***
Addison-Wesley Publishing Company • 2725 Sand Hill Road • Menlo, CA 94025
These manuals give instructions for teaching basic concepts essential to mathematics through manipulatives and discovery. The first covers concepts normally taught in K-2 such as patterns, counting, graphing, place value, and application of principles plus much more. Uses beans and cups and common things around the house. Not updated since the seventies, the pictures are out-of-date, but the children never see these since this is a teacher's manual. 3-6 skills are covered in ***Mathematics...A Way of Thinking*** through the patterns of addition, subtraction, multiplication, division, fractions, decimals, measurement, metrics, probability, logic, and problem solving.

Math-U-See by Steven Demme.
Math-U-See • 1378 River Road • Drumore, PA 17518-9760
1-888-854-MATH (6284) • http://.www.MathUSee.com
I'm quite impressed with this concept and think it will give a jump start to anyone who is failing because of a lack of understanding of place value. This program features a good compromise between worksheets and manipulatives, with emphasis on understanding and use of concepts in story problems. The author is incredible with kids and math concepts. You may choose either a secular or Christian musical skip counting tape. The Christian is the best I've seen. Designed for home use, the video introduction assists student and teacher. Additional practice will be needed. It is amazing how few children really understand place value and how essential that concept is to mathematical thinking.

Miquon Math

Key Curriculum Press • P.O. Box 2304 • Berkeley, CA 94702
This program is a good compromise between worksheets and manipulatives. It uses Cuisenaire® rods for instruction, then transfers information to worksheets. The emphasis is on learning the manipulation of numerals (writing a concept many ways). The inversion of problems (7+? = 9 and ?x2=60) will drive most special needs children absolutely crazy (and their teacher if she insists they figure it out without the rods!). I love the charts which show the patterns of the multiplication tables! I think this is better for gifted or at least average thinkers, but does incorporate enough room for your special needs student to work the problems if they can understand the format. Personally, I don't like the Cuisenaire rods, but many do.

Moving With Math

Math Teacher's Press • 5100 Gamble Drive • Minneapolis, MN 55416
This program is diagnostic (helps you determine what your child doesn't know), prescriptive (gives you what you need to teach missing skills), and systematic. It is relatively inexpensive (especially if you already have the manipulatives gathering dust on the shelf or have several children coming up). Daily reviews (spiral curriculum) are provided which are separate from the worksheets practicing today's skills (sequential curriculum). The worksheets are not too cluttered, though a few children will have trouble writing in the space provided. The program provides for preschool through pre-algebra and nothing seems to be left out. Teacher script is given for those who desire that. Concepts are reinforced through manipulatives, games, and worksheets. Adequate practice is included. The authors suggest you spend approximately one

Moving With Math , continued

hour per day (10 minutes review, 30 minutes activity, 15 minutes independent work) on math. Levels A-D rather than grades 1-8 (each level covers two grades) make it appropriate for the student to move at his own pace without fear of being in an inappropriate grade level. Additional children cost only $10 per year. Changing ten units to one ten is taught with a magician. As good as it is, every program has drawbacks: 1. This program is really to be used one on one. 2. It will take more than one hour of your time daily - for one subject with one child. It is **comprehensive** and demands that kind of time. 3 The system will take some figuring out.

Old Fashioned Products, Al and Sue Schuler

4860 Burnt Mountain Rd. • Ellijay, GA 30540
800-962-8849 • FAX: 1-706-635-7611 or -7672

These marvelous instructive math manipulative games do more than give math practice; consistent frequent play will enable children to internalize concepts. Different components range from preschool through high school! You may want to start with easier games even for older children who have not understood concepts. Optional marble or write-on-board format. For children with fine motor problems, use write-ons or they'll lose their marbles! I love the Number Neighbors designed for younger children with little "trains" and 1" marbles. You can teach everything from sequence, counting, place value with them and more with this beginner's program. All the games would be a great companion to any math program. The higher levels challenge me more than I want to admit, but kids seem to eat them up. Be sure to start out at a level which is easy and don't increase in difficulty until the child is really ready!

Professor B

P.O. Box 2079 Duluth, GA 30096
800-VIP-MATH • 770-814-8888 • 770-814-8899
http://www.profb.com • email: profbent@aol.com

Designed by a mathematician with a love for the Lord, this unique approach seeks to discard rote memorization as a way of learning basic arithmetic and to develop thinking skills that allow children to make mathematical computations automatically. Praised by newspapers, recognized by the United Nations, rescuing children from humdrum pages of drilling facts, this method may teach YOU concepts you never understood!

Golden Step Up Series (Available at discount stores)

With all the "stuff" on the market, these workbooks are the ones I used with my special needs children in a private school. (Of course I did lots of real life, hands-on experiences and provided extra instruction and practice as well.) They don't provide enough practice in some areas and have some offensive pictures and magic themes (I cut away the problems), but the general structure of the program is sound and they are inexpensive and readily available at your local discount store!

Saxon Math

Traditional spiral curriculum with small incremental steps which seems to be the choice of many for the junior and senior high. Requires copying of problems which is often difficult for special needs children. Many children can almost teach themselves math with Saxon; others can't handle the amount of work or the constant switching from one concept to another.

Touch Math, by **Innovative Learning Concepts, Inc**.
6760 Corporate Drive • Colorado Springs, Colorado 80919-1999
http://www.touchmath.com
This is the best program I've seen for severe special needs children with difficulty writing and/or transferring from manipulatives to paper and pencil, **but** they've packaged it for schools and its prices reflect that. It does a very good job of bridging the gap between manipulatives and worksheets. The company has incorporated both repetition and touching into learning the concepts of numbers. Numeral one has one dot, two has two dots, etc. The dots are built into the numeral and easy to remember and revisualize. This program teaches using the dots for everything from counting to multiplication and division. Very clear worksheets leave plenty of space for answers. Multiplication charts included in the multiplication kit are absolutely wonderful! Appropriate even for fairly severely handicapped children (Down's and motor impaired), this may be the choice of the day for math for the developmentally delayed learner. It is a secular company and I haven't seen it all, but the only offensive thing I've seen is one wizard on one worksheet. Some children may become addicted to using the counters built into the numerals and have trouble working without them, but many of them might not be able to work without them at all. Unfortunately, the actual materials are definitely designed for school situations and costly for individual use. There is a video which demonstrates the most important features of the program and is available for a 30-day free viewing. Try viewing the video to learn how the touch points work in all phases of math. Then decide if it's worth it for your situation.

Chapter Fourteen

Points to Consider
When Choosing
A Reading Method

Preparation needed and **expense** are two factors in choosing a reading program about which I'm sure you are concerned. If your child has some special needs to consider, however, there are other points which you consider. Even if your child excels at memorization, there should be some **understanding of concepts** and **principles** which can be applied in more than one situation. Your child will need a **systematic**, orderly presentation of concepts in a **context** in which he can more readily remember and apply the principles you are teaching. The approach should be **multi-sensory**, incorporating as many of the senses and learning styles as possible, while providing **alternate methods of practice,** and responding for the child who has difficulty with a see-say-and-write approach. **Music or rhythm** is usually an advantage, but when overdone can be a distraction. **Mnemonics** (catchy phrases, alliteration, acronyms and so on which aid the memory) are helpful for many children. **Humor, body involvement,** and **games** are beneficial for most types of learners. For special needs children, it is especially important that there be a **flexible pace** and a simple method of **evaluating** when they are ready to move on. Stress, tension, and discomfort impede the learning process. A comfortable, child-friendly, yet structured and sequential presentation, is essential for special needs children.

Be wary of programs that teach all short vowel sounds at once, especially if they do it in alphabetical order. When you teach in that sequence, you present short I and short E at the same time or in sequence. Most children under seven or eight don't hear the difference. (In our lazy speech there often **is** no difference at all!) When you present them in this order, you create a problem. I have found it better to present them in a different sequence and to teach children to read and spell. Teach short A first and then play games with words which have only short A. When they are proficient with these, add words with short I. When this is simple, add words with O, then U and last of all E. Both *Scaredy Cat Reading System* (my own system) and *Primary Phonics* (by Educators Publishing Service) present the vowels this way which is successful with most children, including special needs.

When your child is beginning to read, it is sometimes difficult to find books that are simple enough to ensure success. Be careful not to limit the child's exposure at this time to what he can read independently! Continue reading aloud to him until he is reading aloud to his own children! When you come to a word he should be able to read, point to it and let him say the word. Then when he is reading aloud to you and he comes to a word he does not know, he points to it and you say it aloud. This keeps the flow smooth and aids comprehension. Do not force your child to struggle with an unfamiliar word when he is reading for information or pleasure. That breaks continuity and makes it difficult to concentrate on content. Keep "sounding out" to your reading instruction time. If reading is not a pleasure, the child will not do it for fun. In choosing a book for fun, have the child count the words he cannot read on a page. If the average is more than five, the book is too difficult for him to tackle alone. Read it with him or choose another book.

Easy readers can be found in the library and bookstores. Ask for "easy readers" or "beginning readers" or "Step Into Reading™" books. **Bluestocking Press** has the best selection I've ever seen. **God's World Book Club, Educators Publishers Service, DLM,** and **Modern Curriculum Press** are other sources. If your older student is uncomfortable reading "baby books," let him know that many adults read juvenile fiction for fun. Help him understand the difference between enjoyment reading and reading instruction! Look for easy-to-read biographies.

If you try several programs, the third one will probably work well. By the third time around, your child is able to grasp the concepts no matter how they are introduced, as they are really applying all the accumulated knowledge of all three methods – and he is older as well. For best success, choose a program that both you and the child are comfortable with.

Please let me admit up front that I am very prejudiced concerning reading programs. I looked for over 10 years to find something that worked with my "failure-oriented reluctant learners." Every method had severe limitations or drawbacks. I knew that God wrote a book. He is not capricious, deciding that some can learn to read and others should not. If He wrote a book, His desire was that **everyone** be able to read it. When I found nothing that worked, I spent over 10 years developing the stories which now provide the foundation of *The Scaredy Cat Reading System.* It incorporates the best of many programs and matches with the skills and deficits of "special learners." It has been successful, as well, with average and gifted learners. I've tried to be as objective as I can and present only what I know from my experience, but I admit my prejudice.

While I am at it, let me mention one other thing. Some of us are "turned off" when we see that a particular material was designed for the learning disabled. We don't have any children **like that!** We look elsewhere. But the truth is if it works with learning disabled students, it is some of the best material on the market! **What the learning disabled need** is the very best teaching methods combined with a variety of methods of review, consistent small doses of practice and lots of built-in features to keep them interested over the long haul. What child wouldn't be blessed by that?

Chapter Fifteen

Chart Comparing Some Popular Reading Methods

SCRS = Scaredy Cat Reading System
100E = One Hundred Easy Lessons
ALA = At Last A Reading Method for Everyone!
HRR = Home Run Reading
TIC = Tutoring Is Caring

WRTR = Writing Road to Reading
HOF = Hooked on Phonics
SSR = Sing, Spell, Read and Write
AP = Alpha Phonics
PAT = Play and Talk

Program	SCRS	WRTR	100E	ALA	HOF	SSR	HRR	AP	TIC	PAT
Preparation	2	3	1	1	1	2	1	1	3	1
Expense	$$	$$	$	$$	$$$	$$$	$$$	$	$	$$$
Systematic	1	1	3	1	3	2	1	1	1	1
Multi-Sensory	1	3	3	3	3	2	2	3	1	2
Comfortable	1	3	2	1	2	2	1	2	1	1
Context	1	0	0	0	0	3	2	0	0	0
Music, Rhythm	1	0	0	0	*	**	2	0	0	2
Humor	1	0	0	?	0	2	1	0	2	2
Body, Movement	1	0	0	0	0	2	0	0	2	?
Big Picture	1	0	0	0	0	0	0	0	0	0
Flexible Pace	1	2	0	2	1	1	2	1	1	2
Sequence/Vowels	1 at a time	All	?	All	?	LONG SHORT	1	1	?	?
Spelling	1	1?	?	?	0	?	2	?	?	1
Mnemonics	1	?	0	?	0	?	0	0	0	?
Games	1	0	?	?	0	2	0	0	1	1
Other	Mastery Logical Christian Friendly	Much writing, Guessing game	Untruths Sight method Inexpensive	Good work sheets	Rap music Boring practice	Loses organization Has readers	Workbook, has audios	Inexpensive	Inexpensive	Most expensive

1 = excellent   2 = average   3 = poor   4 = negative   0 = does not include   ? = I don't know
* Rhythm is Rap music and related only to practice, not to understanding
**Songs so similar as to cause confusion

Bonus Box

Books on Dyslexia

The Gift of Dyslexia by Ron Davis
Perigee Books • ISBN 0-399-52293-X

Uncommon Gifts by James Evans ISBN 0-877-888493

Web Sites

http://www.greenwood.org
Dyslexia, Learning Disabilities and Literary Resource Site
School for Boys ages 10-16 and Homeschool assistance

http://www.avko.org
Audio-Visual-Kinesthetic-Organization
Dyslexic author has help for learning to read and spell

http://www.bda-dyslexia.org.uk/
British Dyslexia Association
Helps and resources

http://www.interdys.org
International Dyslexia Association

http://www.texthelp.com
Computerized assistance with spelling and grammar

Chapter Sixteen

Comparisons of Reading Programs

The reading programs which seem to have had most success with special needs children are
Explode the Code , The Scaredy Cat Reading System and *Writing Road to Reading.*
Explode the Code is a series of workbooks which may be helpful for children who need phonics
presented through the visual mode. It is practice with little or no instruction. *The Scaredy Cat
Reading System* works well with children who seek meaning, enjoy variety, movement, and
games, learn readily through songs and stories, and can learn to apply principles they understand
to many situations. It requires parent/teacher involvement, preparation of games and materials,
and teacher flexibility of pace and presentation. *Writing Road to Reading* is helpful for children
who thrive in a very structured situation with much detail and great emphasis on writing. It is
difficult for children who cannot tolerate detail, long periods of sitting, memorization without
meaning, and/or emphasis on fine motor practice.

AlphaPhonics by Sam Blumenfeld

This program is well sequenced with much repetition. There are very complete word lists and
some helpful sentence lists. It does not teach the rules, give any methods or understanding of
why, or give teaching methods or practice materials other than word and sentence lists. What
you do with those lists is left up to you.

ABeka

ABeka Book Publications • Box 18000 • Pensacola, FL 32532 • 800-874-2352
This system tends to build either great readers or non-readers. All the short vowels are
introduced at once in a sequence which leads to confusion for children with auditory processing
problems. It practices untruths temporarily (for example, *be* is pronounced "beh" when first
introduced). It teaches a sample word for each letter sound or cluster of sounds, and assumes that
the child can then recognize that sound wherever he sees it. There is much oral repetition with no
understanding of **why**. It does provide some good readers (texts). Others I found offensive, with
fairy tales for the young children and "Emperor's New Clothes" for fourth graders who are very
sensitive about nudity. Originally designed for classroom use, this curriculum requires much
preparation and tends to be expensive when all the texts and teacher's manuals are purchased.
With several children at different levels, it becomes nearly impossible to manage.

At Last A Reading Method for Every Child! by Mary Pecci
A wide variety of excellent worksheets accompany this teacher-created program. The only drawback I saw in this one was the presentation of all short and long vowel sounds at once. This usually leads to confusion. It has good instruction to the teacher, is cheap and thorough.

Bob Jones University Press

Bob Jones University Press • Greenville, SC 29614
This curriculum teaches some understanding of **why** through little stories with each new phonics rule. There are wonderful readers at all levels. Comprehension and discernment are stressed. In the early lessons, so many stories about different phonics rules may become confusing. Designed for classroom use, this becomes expensive when all the texts, readers, writing materials, and teacher's manuals are purchased.

Primary Phonics and *Explode the Code*
Educators Publishers Service • 75 Moulton Street • Cambridge, MA 02138-1104
Both of these programs are largely phonics through a visual workbook presentation. They work well with children who are deaf or have auditory processing problems and for parents who prefer a structured workbook approach. I haven't really been able to figure out the difference between *Primary Phonics* and *Explode the Code*. *Primary Phonics* workbooks and readers make an excellent supplement for *The Scaredy Cat Reading System* as they follow the same sequence of introducing the vowels. **EPS (Educators Publishers Service)** has other products which are excellent for special needs children including phonetic readers and materials on vocabulary development. They are quite inexpensive - even more so if you can find five friends who want the same book as they have a discount for six or more of any single item.

Home Run Reading
Colorful, expensive, glorified workbooks join with a cute baseball theme on audio tapes. Some of the poems and literature included on the tapes contain content which is offensive to some Christians. It has some silly rhymes and riddles to enhance memory and includes teaching of some comprehension. This child-friendly program may enable some children to learn to read without any attention from an adult.

Hooked On Phonics
Gateway Educational Products, Ltd. • 1045 W. Katella Ave. Ste. 200 • Orange, CA 92667
The best thing about this program is its advertising! From there it falls seriously below standards. Rap music practice of sounds and words, workbooks which are rows and rows of syllables or words with no meaning, and no understanding at all of concepts or rules are some of the major drawbacks. It's worked for some kids, but I wouldn't waste my money. Requires no preparation, has many audio tapes. This very expensive program is mindless practice of sounds.

Laguna Beach Educational Books

245 Grandview • Laguna Beach, CA 92651
714-494-4225
Dr. Edward Fry has written several textbooks on reading and devised the "Fry Readability Scale." *How to Teach Reading,* gives you pointers to enhance any "program" you are using and includes a simple comprehension test to enable you to determine your child's reading level.

Learning Language Arts Through Literature by Debbie Strayer
The first grade learn-to-read program (based on Ruth Beechick's approach) includes puppets, fun readers, and dice games. The later levels (2nd-7th grade) cover all language arts skills through reading selections reprinted from real books and focusing on skills which can be found in each. I'd skip the second grade level for most children unless they are immature. Some children will need more specific teaching of language arts skills (Try F.L.A.G.G.S. See Language Arts Section), and then use this for review in later grades.

Lockhart Reading System, Inc (Formerly known as Char L or Intensive Phonics)
1420 Lockhart Drive • Suite 211 • Kennesaw, GA 30144 •770-428-6796 • FAX 770-419-1900 • 800-501-6767 • www.lockhart-reading.com • EMAIL: info@lockhart-reading.com
"The programs...build a foundation first by teaching the 42 sounds of the alphabet and the Lockhart 5 phonetic skills." It then builds step by step in a no nonsense way.

Love and Learning
P.O. Box 4088 Dearborn, MI 48126-4088
This reading program uses video, audio and workbook to teach very young children or severe special needs children and adults. There are six kits. The first teaches the alphabet and one associated word for each letter such as A for apple and b for bus. The second introduces 50 common words such as arm, button, shoe. It is basically a sight approach with some phonics concepts incorporated. It emphasizes functional words and developing some basic language structure. Also available from NATHHAN.

One Hundred Easy Lessons
Several pages of intensive phonics are presented in the instructions to parents, but sight approach is used for teaching the children. It practices untruths temporarily (for instance reading and writing sentences with no capital letters for twenty lessons before capitals are introduced) and teaches no understanding of why. This program tells the instructor exactly what to say every day, using one lesson a day. It's inexpensive and requires no preparation.

Reading Made Easy by Valerie Bendt
108 scripted lessons proceed from letter sounds to reading two syllables and covers through about second grade phonics in 512 pages. Additional phonics "rules" such as (tion: nation, creation) and (ful: joyful, playful) are listed at the end of the manual. It begins with the short a sound and introduces words through word endings such as *ap, am, ad, at,* and *ag*. The first words (all ending in *ap*) are read in Lesson 9. Italics is used for reading and strongly suggested for writing. Three lessons a week with review in between is the suggested approach, though fewer are recommended for young or struggling learners. Most lessons introduce one to three new sounds (such as bold **o** in snow and *ow* as in *cow*. Sentences are made without a capitol letter (in lessons 11-14) until a capitol T is introduced in Lesson 15. At first, the child reads with the help of print clues (such as gray letters represent short vowel sounds, bold letters represent long vowels, dotted letters represent silent letters and combinations of letters which make one sound are circled). First stories are very simple and have a picture and discussion to allow for some maturity of thinking beyond the very beginning reading level.

Reading Milestones
Edmark • Box 3218 • Redmond, WA 98073-3218 • 800-362-2890
I haven't seen this one, but it is recommended for hearing impaired and deaf children. Eight levels of instruction go from non-reader to approximately fourth grade.

Scaredy Cat Reading System by Joyce Herzog
800-745-8212 • www.joyceherzog.com
Phonics rules told within the context of a single story enhance memory and understanding. Introduced with Songs; learned through reasoning; understood and remembered through stories; reinforce through games and activities; master step by step. Teaches logical thinking skills at the same time as learning to read. Includes some comprehension, but encourages the reading of real books. Language skills through second grade level is built into Beginner's and Advanced Beginner's books (Level Two and Three). This program requires intensive parent/child involvement which is the single most important ingredient of learning to read! In all likelihood, the teacher will learn as much as the student with this child-friendly and homeschool-friendly program. Builds spelling with reading skill. Compatible with unit study approach and most adaptable program available. Optional Christian components.

Sing, Spell, Read and Write
This program has songs and a limited number of games to practice skills. The sequence is short vowels, then long vowels. After that, the remaining sounds are presented with no specific order. Some children become confused by the sameness of the songs. Rules as such are not taught.

Writing Road To Reading
Teaches all the sounds of each letter (vertical phonics) and more than 70 "phonograms" (sound/letter association) through writing and drill. Works well with some kids. Very difficult for children with fine motor problems, short attention span, or a desire for fun and meaning. Though it claims to be "multi-sensory," it is simply see, say, and write. If your child can stand heavy amounts of writing, much repetition, learning many bits of information, and a guessing game to put the pieces together, this is right for you. The kids I know who learned this way still can't spell. Most people need *Teaching Reading at Home* or a 16-hour workshop to understand how to implement this program.

Chapter Seventeen

How to Interest a Child in Reading

• Read to your child from the womb until he is reading to his own children. It is never too soon - or too late - to begin!

• Make a difference between the process of learning to read or developing reading skill and reading for fun or information. When your child is reading for fun or information, he should read a book that is below his instructional level and he should not be required to sound out or struggle with words. At that time, tell him any word he needs with no criticism, clues, or struggle. Save the sounding out and struggling for reading instruction time.

• Differentiate between oral reading and silent reading. Some children with reading problems will never be good oral readers, but can read successfully if not required to pronounce the words.

• Let your child see you:
   Reading for information
   Using the dictionary when you need to for pronunciation or meaning
   Reading for enjoyment

• Read the humor in *Reader's Digest* and laugh. Occasionally tell what you are laughing about. Other times say, "Oh, you'll have to read this one for yourself!"

• Read wonderful short stories to your children. *Guideposts* is full of treasures (see magazine resources).

• Begin reading aloud a story, novel, or biography (at your children's reading level) to your children. Stop at a very important part and lay the book down in plain sight. Don't find the time to finish it.

• Choral reading is fun. Read aloud together poems, Psalms, familiar rhyming books, and scripture.

• When you are reading aloud to your child and you come to a word he can easily read, point to it and have him say it. Then you continue reading with no hesitation. When your child reads aloud to you and comes to a word he doesn't know, he can point to it and you supply the word. Keep "sounding out" only for reading instruction time, not when reading for fun or information.

• Read aloud **good** picture books even to older children. Read one several days in a row and discuss, draw a picture, do an activity, reenact, do a related project or field trip.

• Many of us improved our reading ability when we read the words to songs in church.

• Play word games and spelling games. Do crossword puzzles and other word puzzles.

• Get computer games which require reading.

• Make a list of words learned, books read, or other achievements.

• Read every other paragraph with your child reading the one in between. If that is too much of a challenge, you read two pages to his paragraph. Keep the flow. Enjoy the time you spend together. If it is a drag, you won't be as consistent and consistency is necessary for improvement!

• Spend 15 minutes every day playing a game with words or sentences.

• Encourage progress. "I think you're getting better!" "I can see progress every day!" "This seems to be getting easier for you!" "I'm glad you're sticking with this. It'll get easier soon." "You really make me proud!"

Chapter Eighteen

Teaching Reading Comprehension

Give a purpose for reading:

Short Term

What does the story mean?

Why was it written?

Does the author communicate:

well?   the truth?   precisely?

What information is presented? Is it:

truthful?   helpful?   useful?   uplifting?

Long Term

Learn to read because God wrote a book.

Learn to read to obtain useful information.

Learn to read to expand one's understanding of the world around.

Learn to read signs in our world (restroom, danger, road signs, etc.)

Learn to read to communicate (notes, letters, etc.)

Learn to read to become employable.

Learn to read to obtain a driver's license.

Characterization:

Name and describe the most important character(s).

Name and describe the supporting character(s).

Are the characters believable?

Are the characters portrayed exemplary and good role models?

Are the characterizations precise enough to be trusted?

Setting:

Decide if the story is fact or fiction, nonsense or realistic.

Describe the physical setting of the story.

Describe the geographical setting of the story.

Describe the emotional setting of the story.

Describe the social setting of the story.

Describe the historical time setting of the story.

Plot:

> What situation(s) confronted the hero(ine)?
> What was the response of the hero(ine)?
> What problems were resolved in the story?
> What problems were left unresolved?

Moral:

> What lessons are to be learned from the story?
> Are the lessons taught true to Scripture?

Additional Information:

> Note the subtle details of information presented. Are they:
>> helpful to the plot? truthful? useful to life?

Presentation:

> Is it grammatically correct?
> Is the language precise enough to communicate accurately?
> Are the details of the setting accurate?
> Is there a lack of extraneous and distracting clutter in the plot and characteriztation?

Chapter Nineteen
Teaching Discernment in Literature

Evaluating Fiction and Biographies

It isn't enough to teach the skill of reading alone, we must teach the student to evaluate what he reads. Here are questions that guide deeper thinking and discernment and encourage your student to take responsibility for his learning and actions. How do the actions, attitudes, decisions and actions of the characters line up with Biblical standards?

God: (The Supreme Authority)
  Where is God in this work?

  How is God presented?

personal	impersonal	caring	everyone
sovereign	everything	holy	just
universal	triune	distant	loving
illusory	omnipotent	inconsistent	distant
created	Creator	creative	knowable
interested	fallen	dead	a force
finite	infinite	transcendent	good
evil	moral	changing	part of me

How is information about God handled?

Who are the messengers of God?

How do the messengers of God communicate?

What would God think about this work?

Man: (people in the story)

- How are characters developed?

- Are the characters strong or wishy-washy?

- Which of the characters does the author want you to like?

What are their character traits?
Are they:

loving	kind	thoughtful	stable
helpful	honest	just	loyal
caring	truthful	cautious	enthusiastic
involved	peacemakers	giving	forgiving
wise	maturing	obedient	thrifty
respectful	resourceful	gentle	reverent
grateful	responsible	alert	flexible
diligent	prayerful	enduring	hospitable
patient	positive	punctual	sensitive
wise	content	creative	thorough
decisive	sincere	orderly	meek
joyful	generous	available	persuasive
spiritual	respectful	self-controlled	

Which of the characters does the author want you to not like?
What are their character traits?
Are they

self-serving	wasteful	harsh	rash
cruel	unreliable	restless	apathetic
thoughtless	lazy	indifferent	rejecting
careless	inconsistent	unthankful	extravagant
anxious	disrespectful	willful	callused
impure	covetous	judgmental	under-achievers
vacillators	hypocritical	disorganized	angry
rude	proud	deceitful	full of self-pity
stingy	contentious	selfish	self-indulgent

How did the hero(ine) treat:

authority	evil	friends	truth
elderly people	goodness	animals	handicapped people
enemies	children	work	women

How (and how well) did the characters in the book communicate their:

feelings	frustrations
values	convictions
preferences	loyalties

How does the hero(ine) (villain, authorities, parents) handle

fear	stress	sexual advances	frustration
failure	opportunity	success	grief
loss	adversity	challenge	disappointments
fame	pain	spiritual matters	achievement

Which of the characters did you identify with (feel close to)? Why?
Which of the characters did you want to avoid (punish, etc.)?
How well prepared was the hero(ine) to handle what he faced?
How had the hero(ine) prepared himself to handle what he faced?

The World: (earthly people and forces outside of self)
What hidden assumptions underly the text?
What type of government is idealized?
What laws are proposed, supposed, and honored?

Authority: (the power to enforce obedience, position to influence, the people who do both)
Who or what influences thinking and behavior of the characters?
How is authority represented?
Who is shown to be the authority?
How are readers encouraged to respond to authority?
To whom do the characters go for advice and leadership?

Truth: (real, unchanging facts or principles)
How is truth defined?
What questions are asked?
How are the questions answered?
By what authority are the questions answered?
What is the position of the one answering the questions?
Who is asking the questions?
What questions are left unanswered?
What other questions should have been asked?

Values: (worth or importance)
What goals are set, encouraged, attained, thwarted?
What values are rewarded?
What attitudes are shown?
How are the young, the old, and the infirmed treated?
What activities are encouraged?
Is the general attitude of the book hopeful or one of despair?

What things are valued?

time	friendships	money	possessions
comfort	work	joy	lack of conflict
eternity	prayer	Bible	books
learning	education	happiness	sex
love	ambition	success	sorrow
faith	recreation	acquisition	achievement
service	fulfillment	knowledge	wisdom

What is the theme of the story?
Is it uplifting?

pure	holy	just	of good report
true	noble	right	admirable
excellent	praiseworthy		

Ethics: (standards of right and wrong, moral principles which guide)
How is evil treated?

laughed at	admired	jokes made about
punished	with horror	as a challenge to overcome

How are problems handled?
What solutions are offered?
Who is rewarded in the book? (with good or evil)
Did they earn their reward?
Did God's grace prevail?
Do you want to be like them?
What is the moral of the book? Is it a godly one?
What lessons were learned by the people in the book?

Personal Response:
How would you have reacted differently if you had faced one of the situations of the book?

Would you (or anyone) recommend this book to your:

mother	father	sister	brother
best friend	worst enemy	Sunday School teacher	
grandmother	grandfather	favorite aunt	

Would you rather have seen a different:
ending
response of the hero(ine)
problem

Would you feel uneasy if your sister (brother) were close friend to the hero(ine)?
If the author wrote another book about this person, would you want to read it? Why?

Chapter Twenty

Developing Written Expression

If your child is struggling with written expression, try some real life writing in small doses.

• Take pictures of the student involved in a sequential task such as making a garden, preparing a meal, or doing a science project. Have the student arrange the pictures in sequence and label each one with a complete sentence.

• Cut apart the sentences or paragraphs of a story. Have the student rearrange them and read them aloud. See if it changed the meaning. Have the student put them back into the correct order.

• Give the student incomplete sentences to finish such as, "I wish I...", or "One day the cat...", or "When I am 16, I hope to..."

• Make a squiggle on a blank paper. Have the student make it into a picture of something. Then have him write three sentences about what he drew.

• Each day, together, write a story telling what you did or what you plan to do.

• Encourage the student to make lists of things to remember.

• Let the student dictate a story to you. Type it or print it. Let him copy it in his handwriting or on the computer. Allow him to add details and illustrations.

• Have the student keep a diary or journal. Provide as much help as he desires spelling words and forming thoughts into sentences. In this situation it is all right to accept incomplete sentences.

• Encourage the child to have a pen pal or write letters to a grandparent or cousin.

• Start a spelling file. Use a 3x5 filing box system. Each time the student needs help spelling a word, have him bring you the card for the beginning sound of the word. See if he can tell you the first three letters. If he cannot, provide them for him. With these three letters, he can successfully look up the word in a dictionary and write it on the card for the next time he needs it.

• Have the student write to companies and ask for samples of their products or literature explaining how their products are made. Create letterhead stationary to make these requests.

• By age ten or so teach keyboarding skills, especially to a child who still struggles with handwriting.

• Allow and encourage use of word processor, especially for an older learner who continues to struggle.

• Encourage your student to write thank you letters to people who have influenced his life.

• Have your student draw pictures of a place you have visited, or the steps in a project he has completed. Then have him compose a sentence to describe each picture. Combine the sentences into paragraphs to have a complete story.

• Teach the student to use resources such as telephone books, dictionaries, encyclopedias, atlases, maps, charts, and globes.

• Teach the student to take notes by writing on a 3x5 card three words to summarize an idea or paragraph. Have him copy the book title, publisher, page number, etc on the card. Then have him shuffle and organize the cards into an outline of a report. Have him write a report from his notes.

• Have the student start a dictionary of favorite family phrases or insider's jokes.

• Have the student address envelopes for you and do other real life writing tasks.

• Have the student keep a prayer or hospitality journal.

• Provide opportunity for the student to observe people he respects writing.

• Provide experiences for the student to write about. Compose stories or reports together.

• Allow the student to tape record his ideas before he writes.

• Encourage the writing of notes to inform, encourage, and praise.

We learn to write by writing.

Think of ways to incorporate writing into normal daily life so that the student will see the importance of it while he gains experience in using it!

Chapter Twenty One
Looking at Language Arts

F.L.A.G.G.S., Letz Farmer
(FUNdamental Language Arts Games Supplement)
Mastery Publications • 90 Hillside Lane • Arden, NC 28704 • 704-684-0429
This is a marvelous package of games (printed on cardstock and ready to cut and assemble game pieces) to practice all the language arts skills grades 1-4. There is no better way to learn language skills than through games. At a bargain price, this is a treasure! Kids love it!

Ellen Hajek (formerly Hajek House) has written helpful language materials. Her publishing company has broken up and her products are available from several different companies. *See It and Spell It!* Is available through Perron SOI Center • 303-691-0882. The *Humpties* series does for parts of speech what *Scaredy Cat* does for reading and is available through **Builder Books** • 446 Pharr Road • Riverside, WA 98849 • 1-509-826-6021. *Humpties – Parts of Speech with "Eggceptional" Personalities* turns the parts of speech into little egg-shaped characters who help you remember their functions. *Building Sentences with the Humpies* continues through explaining subjects, predicates, objects and an introduction to diagramming. *The "How to Write" Book* is an introduction to writing from paragraphs to reports and can be obtained through **Teaching and Learning Company** • 204 Buchanan Street • P.O. Box 10 • Carthage, IL 62321-0010 • 800-852-1234.

How to Teach Spelling/Vocabulary From the Bible
Lowell and Deborah Tukua • 7009 Corning Road • Iron City, TN 38463
Great little booklet explaining how to take the child's lessons directly from the Bible at three levels (K-1st grade, 2nd-3rd grade, 4th-5th grade).

Learning Grammar Through Writing
Educators Publishing Service, Inc. • 75 Moulton Street • Cambridge, MA 02138
Once your student has learned basic mechanics of writing, this book is a wonderful tool! You mark the error in the child's own writing. He looks up the appropriate page and corrects his own errors. It is best used about fifth grade through high school.

Learning Language Arts Through Literature by Debbie Strayer
See description on pages 52-3.

Choosing and Using Curriculum

God's Gift of Language B, Oral Language Exercises, and ***The Case of the Missing Part of Speech*** **ABeka Book** • Pensacola, FL 32423-9160 • 800-874-2352
God's Gift of Language B has the best step-by-step teaching I've ever seen on how to do a research report. If your child has reached junior or senior high without developing this important skill, this would be a fine resource. Don't expect them to do the rest of the chapters in the book. *Oral Language Exercises* is wonderful for practicing correctly spoken English. Most children who use poor grammar do so because they are accustomed to hearing incorrect usage. This builds in practice with correct grammar and develops listening skills at the same time. Originally designed as a musical assembly program, *The Case of the Missing Part of Speech* provides delightful songs for the parts of speech. Your children will love learning and really understand the parts of speech with this cassette. Who knows, maybe your support group could put on the play and everyone would have a great time!

Information Please by Pat Wesolowski
D. P. & K. • 1285 Morgan Springs Road • Dayton, TN 37321 • 423-570-7172
Wonderful 20 questions worksheets at three levels to teach research skills.

Miller Pads and Paper, Randy and Renee Miller
2840 Neff Road • Boscobel, WI 53805 • 608-375-2181
Inexpensive source of all kinds of writing papers. Write for catalog!

Pencil Playground by Jeanne Mulligan
Estella Graphics • RR 3, Box 369 Montrose, PA 18801-8842
www.pencilplayground.com
I am often asked how to encourage writing skills in young or special needs children. This program will do just that. Instructions are simple and straightforward and broken down into small steps to encourage participation and completion. Brainstorming comes first and is enhanced with cute drawings. Writing sentences is next. Then the sentences are cut apart, organized, shuffled and rearranged to be copied in a logical structural sequence. Lessons have enough similarity to be comfortable with, enough variety to hold interest.

66

Chapter Twenty Two

Comparison of Handwriting Styles

Many people are switching to *Italic* or *D'Nealian* handwriting programs for a less traumatic transfer to cursive as the chart below indicates. *D'Nealian* is a compromise between italic and cursive in that it uses some capital cursive forms. The *Getty/Dubay Italic Series* is an italics handwriting program. Its capital letters look more like manuscript than cursive. Both use a traditional approach of look, trace, and copy.

One thing to keep in mind: the child should still learn to **read** traditional cursive in order to be able to read letters and historical documents which were written in the traditional way.

Program	Letter **Shape** Changes Manuscript to Cursive **Capitals**	Letter **Shape** Changes Manuscript to Cursive **Lower case**	Letter **Slope** Changes **Manuscript to Cursive**
D'Nealian	18	13	None
Palmer (traditional)	26	26	52
Zaner-Bloser	26	26	52
Getty/Dubay Italic	2	1	None

 Personally, I taught the traditional ball and stick and transitioned to cursive. I used a simple step which I called "connected printing" to transition between one and the other. Every cursive lower case letter starts on the lower line and ends on the middle line. I just had the children begin on the lower line, swing up to the middle line, and print the letter. Then with one continuous motion, they made tails on their printed letters to get back to the middle line. Without lifting their pencil, they could then print the next letter and tail it up to the middle line again. It was quite simple for them to do most letters and simple words. Letters which do NOT lend themselves to this are: b, f, r, s, x, and z. We just wrote words without those letters until it was easy and then taught those letters. Whatever you choose is fine. The child will likely develop his own style when he is between 10 and 12 no matter what you do!

Draw Write Now by Marie Hablitzel and Kim Stitzer
Barker Creek Publishing, Inc. • P.O. Box 2610 • 375 Sigurd Hanson Road • Paulsbo, WA 98370
800-692-5833 • 360-692-5833 • FAX 360-613-2542 • www.barkercreek.com
This wonderful series assumes that your child can already form the letters and needs to practice - and then makes practicing more fun. It gives children drawing lessons (line-by-line, circle-by-circle format) to develop the eye-hand coordination needed for handwriting skills. It was written by a teacher who "saw her second-grade students becoming increasingly frustrated with their drawing efforts and disenchanted with repetitive handwriting drills." Each book coordinates with themes such as The Cold Lands, Fall Topics, and Native Americans.

Handwriting Without Tears by Jan Z Olsen, OTR
8802 Quiet Stream Court • Potomac, MD 20854 • 301-983-8409 • FAX 301-983-6821
http://www.HWTears.com • EMAIL: jan@HWTears.com
Work begins with forming letters with sanded wood blocks and progresses to tracing in the air and using a slate in various ways before pencil and paper are ever used. This helps teach good habits, break old ones, while it eliminates frustration, tears, finger wear and tear, and reversals. Sessions are short and emphasize "doing your best" and working correctly rather than finishing pages. Lots of little tricks assist common problem areas and gentle helpers like kangaroo and helicopter moves make it more fun and interesting. Cursive is vertical rather than slanted and simply taught for success. Remember: short lessons, short practices!

Happy Handwriting by Letz Farmer
Mastery Publications • 90 Hillside Lane Arden • N.C. 28704 • 704-684-0429
This Christian, designed for homeschoolers, program shows several ways of forming each letter including sign language and braille. Cute characters correspond with each of the strokes needed to make traditional ball and stick letters. Lessons include alphabetical order, capitalization, and ordinal numbers. The chart on capitalization is **wonderful!** There could be some problem with too much on a page, but folding the book in order to see only one page at a time will help. The book is bound in such a way as to be accessible by left or right-handed children.

Smithhand© Writing Methods
N11492 Oakwood Road • Daggett, MI 49821 • 906-639-229 • 800-554-4411
Fashioned after the Spencerian cursive of the 1800's, this method is greatly simplified when compared to the Palmer method most of us learned and then rejected in favor of our own invented styles. Designed to flow with the natural movements of the hand, wrist and arms, this is more comfortable and therefore easier to perfect than other methods. You begin instruction when the child can consistently color (using colored pencils) in the direction of the preferred slant. Instructions for formation of letters is brief and straight-forward such as (for letters c, o, and a) "begin these letters slightly below the dashed midline curving upward and to the left to the midline, then downward toward the base line." I believe the cursive method in particular would have benefit for correction problems in older awkward writers.

Zaner-Bloser
1459 King Avenue • Columbus, OH 43216-6764
Special pens, paper and materials to make handwriting easier

Chapter Twenty Three

Geography, History and Science Resources

If you are struggling with a reluctant learner, taking a failing student out of school, or in any way trying to turn burned out kids and/or teachers into happy learners, here is an idea for you. Temporarily drop all "normal" curriculum and textbook studies. Instead, choose a topic like geography of your state, the ocean, or the Civil War and discover the joy of teaching and learning. Get acquainted with your child as together you rediscover the delight of learning. (You can gradually return to some more normal academics, but always keep some learning with the exciting discovery-and-activities method.)

The following resources should make this easy! Turn the neighborhood or indeed the entire United States into your classroom. Write to the Chamber of Commerce of towns you are interested in and ask for free information about their town's history, commerce, and tourist attractions. (That takes care of language arts!) Calculate the distance you'd have to travel to visit, the number of days the trip would take if you traveled 200 miles a day, the gallons of gasoline needed, the cost of the trip, and how long it would take you to save that much money. (There's your math lesson! Even if you do the computing, your child will be learning about the importance of mathematics in our everyday life! Let him use the calculator for this just as you would in real life.) When the literature starts piling in, read it! (Voila! Your reading lesson!) Make some charts or graphs to explain the information you receive. Design a poster ad for one of the parks or businesses. Think of songs related to the area or its history! Begin concentrating on learning instead of covering a curriculum and you and your students will become "happy campers"! You may never return to traditional curricula! Remember textbooks are tools. Do not follow them rigidly, but use them as guides and references. Plan activities. Do projects. Learn from real life. The lessons will be remembered longer, you will enjoy your students more, and they will be instilled with a love for learning that carries them through life!

Geography is a great place to start. Whether you start in your back yard, or studying the countries related to missionaries, Olympic or sports stars, or the daily news, make it come alive by relating it to your children's real life interests. Study a country as if you were planning to visit, determining how many miles you will travel, what transportation means is most feasible, what clothes are appropriate for the climate, time of year to go, and so on. The following tools and companies should give you a great start. Enjoy!

Geography Matters

P.O. Box 92 Nancy, KY 42544 • 800-426-4650
www.geomatters.com • email: geomatters@earthlink.net
These folks specialize in materials to make learning geography and history fun. They are your source for *The Ultimate Geography and Timeline Guide, Uncle Josh's Outline Map Book, Historical Timeline Figures, Mark-It Timeline of History,* a variety of *Mark-It Maps* (laminated outline maps). They also have maps of the world and USA, inflatable globes, accessories to learn states and their capitals and more.

Family Learning Connection, Mark and Janice Vreeland

1934 South 56th Street • West Allis, WI 53219
Wonderful inexpensive ($2-$7) games for every subject (including geography) at every level!

History

is best taught through biographies and real life experiences! Begin with thorough understanding of Biblical history. Teach chronologically. Teach by biographies. Read them aloud in installments. Analyze the behavior of the characters according to scripture (see Teaching Discernment chapter on page 59). Discuss the people and their response to tragedy, triumph, and God. Find easy-to-read biographies for the beginning reader. The *Step Up Series,* available through **Greenleaf Press**, is excellent. Start with the treasure of biographical information in the Bible and tie it all together as you provide the big picture with a timeline. See **Greenleaf Press, Elijah Company**, and **Lifetime Books and Gifts** in the General Resource Section.

History in His Hands by Joyce Herzog
www.joyceherzog.com • 800-745-8212
This series relates both secular and biblical history to the character and nature of God. Volume I covers creation through 6 B.C. Volume II covers 6 B.C. through 1400's A.D. "Read Alouds" give the big picture and Study Guides enable families to dig deeper into the Word as it relates to history. Whether you are trying to piece it all together or give a cohesive picture to your children this is for you!

A Child's History Collection Told in One-Syllable Words
Mantle Ministries •228 Still Ridge • Bulverde, TX 78163
1-877-548-2327 • www.mantlemin.com • email: mantleministries@cs.com
History for the beginning or struggling reader

Science

should be built first on observation of the world through the aspect of seeing the Creator in His creation. You do not need a formal science program before junior high skills are reached. Much information on science can be taught through simple picture books and experiments. There is also a surprising amount of science incorporated in biographies. *The Elijah Company* has wonderful material for teaching science through nature study and real books. Their catalog is an education in itself.

Considering God's Creation is the place to start for elementary students. It takes the Creation story and makes it come alive through simple crafts and cut outs.

The Scientist's Apprentice is the non-scientist's manual for what, why and how to teach science. It is a "one year curriculum," but could well be the means of teaching you how to teach while it does the first year for you. Chapters on astronomy, anatomy, earth science, and oceanography.

Science: The Search (Available through **Cornerstone Curriculum)**
Hands-on approach (K-9) to science and nature with a Christian world view

Thor Unlimited
208 West Hamilton Avenue #290 • State College, PA 16801-5232
888-THOR-321 • 812-234-2144 • FAX 814-234-3452
www.Thor-Unlimited.com • info@Thor-Unlimited.com
"Science toys let you experience the theory"™ Combine fun and learning science with these wonderful learning tools.

Apologia Educational Ministries
1106 Meridian Plaza, Suite 220 • Anderson, IN 46016 • 888-524-4724
Christ-centered junior high and high school science curriculum especially designed for homeschoolers.

Home Training Tools
2827 Buffalo Horn Drive • Laurel, MT 59044-8325 • 800-860-6272
Lab equipment and more

Tobin's Lab
P.O. Box 725 • Culpeper, VA 22701
800-522-4776 • www.tobinlab.com • mike@tobinlab.com
Chemistry sets, anatomy models, science crafts, lab equipment, and more

Nasco Science
901 Janesville Ave. • Fort Atkinson, WI 53538-0901 • 414-563-2446
If it relates to science experiments, they have it!

Bonus Box

Helpful Web Sites:

Here are some web sites that have looked good to me. Please understand: I cannot be responsible for all content or every ad or link you may find, but these seemed safe and helpful.

Christian Missionary biographies http://elvis.rowan.edu/~kilroy/JEK/home.html	**State by State Support Resources** http://eho.org/support/
Print and Learn Worksheets http://www.brobstsystems.com/kids/index.htm	**Index to Graphics on the Internet** http://www.ncrtec.org/picture.htm
Godly Living for Christian Women http://www.bravewc.com/haven/index.html	**Crafts for Kids** http://www.kidsdomain.com
Homeschool Sites http://www.ipl.org/ref/RR/static/edu35.10.00.html	**Children's Museum Online** http://www.hhmi.org/coolscience/
Homeschool Organizations http://www.christianitytoday.com/homeschool/features/hsus.html	**Math Story Problems (Math for Internet Generation)** **Some secular topics** http://www.mathstories.com/index.htm
Learn about the Creator by exploring His creation! http://www.christiananswers.net/kids/home.html	**Ideas for Teachers** http://www.teachingideas.co.uk/
Homeschool Links http://www.jps.net/kgarden/homeschool2/home_school_links.htm	**Religious Resources on the Net** http://www.aphids.com/relres/
Christian Colleges which accept homeschoolers http://www.christianconnector.com/	**Bible Games for upper elementary** http://www.expage.com/page/biblegames
Wow! Make your own games, quiz, test http://www.quia.com/	**Sites researched** http://www.surfnetkids.com/
Homeschool Conferences by State http://www.sound.net/~ejcol/confer.html	**Christlink's Homeschool Links** http://www.christlink.com/hslinks.htm
Typical Course of Study by Grade Level K-12 http://www.worldbook.com/ptrc/html/curr.htm	**The Internet Public Library - a library of web sites!** http://www.ipl.org/ref/
Fun and Learning with World Book Encyclopedia http://www.worldbook.com/fun/html/fun.htm	**Homeschooling on the Cheap** http://www.bcpl.net/~owl/homeschool/

Chapter Twenty Four
Tips for Teaching History

1. Provoke the interest of the student(s):
> Ask an intriguing question.
> Ask a riddle.
> Display something related to the study of_____.
> Show a map of the area where the event took place.
> Display a toy or manipulative related to _____.

2. Lead a discussion.
> Begin with one or two thought provoking questions (see next page).
> End with a list of unanswered questions.

3. Lead the student(s) to do research.
> Provide books at the appropriate reading and interest level.
> Take notes   Draw pictures
> Outline   Create maps
> Study period art, music, costumes, transportation, communication, and weapons.
> Find a game related to the period or happening.

4. Have your student(s) give a report about something they have learned.
> Oral - Share 2-3 important ideas
> Written
>> Choose Topic
>> Outline
>> Rough Draft
>> Reorganize, Second Draft
>> Polish, publish, and present

5. Give additional opportunities to communicate the information learned and studied.

Play	Skit	Chart	Display	Poem
Art	Map	Costume	Diorama	Game
Song	Poster	Mini-Book	List	Oral Reading

ɩ Provoking Questions

ɔu know about_____?

ı._____like_____?

What would it have _____ to have lived _____?
    looked like?   smelled like? sounded like? felt like?

How is _____different from_____?

What have you experienced like_____?

If you were the decision maker, how would you change_____?

How is the <u>climate</u> like_____?
    geography   culture   religion

How is the <u>climate</u> different from _____?
    geography   culture   religion

If Jesus saw _____, how would He respond?

Jonah	Moses	David	Abraham Lincoln
Gandhi	Abraham	Martin Luther King	Mother Theresa
Nathan Hale		Benjamin Franklin	Thomas Edison

What were some of the causes of_____?

List as many effects of _____ as you can.

What would be best about living _____?   worst?

How would your education have been different if you'd lived_____?

How were human relations handled?

What Biblical principles were upheld?   ignored?

Which side would you have wanted to be on?

How would average home life have been like yours?   different from yours?

If you were an <u>artist</u>*, how would you have seen this differently?
    *substitute each of the following:

farmer	chemist	manufacturer	missionary	
store owner	writer	photographer	Christian	nurse or doctor
social worker	teacher	writer	mechanic	mother or father
contractor	millionaire	musician	inventor	shoe salesman

If this event had not happened, how would history have been different?

If this person had not lived, how would history have been different?

If this place had never been found, how would history have been different?

If the car* had (not) been invented then, what would have changed?
   *substitute each of the following:
   wheel   airplane   telephone   scissors

What weapons were common?

What was the chief means of transportation? communication?

How many people were affected by the decision to_____?

If there had been 1,000 more (less) people,* what would have changed?
   *substitute each of the following:
   guns   horses   tanks   newspapers   televisions

If none of the people there could read*, what would have changed?
   *substitute each of the following:
   could talk   could see   could hear   could walk   cared

If all the people had been true Christians*, what would have changed?
   *substitute each of the following:
   millionaires   honest   lazy   careful

Was what the main character did honest*?
   *substitute each of the following:
   truthful   righteous   holy   peaceful
   thoughtful   noble   friendly   carefully thought out

Bonus Box

Books on Autism

Books for children
Russell is Extra Special by Amenta, C., New York, Magination Press, 1992
Please Don't Say Hello by P. Gold, Human Sciences Press/Plenum Publications, 1986
Joey and Sam by Katz, I., and Ritvo, E, Northridge, CA: Real Life Storybooks, 1993

Books for teachers and other interested professionals
The Handbook of Autism A Guide for Parents and Professionals by Aarons, M., and Gittens, T. New York: Tavistock/Routledge, 1992
Autism: Strategies for Change Groden, G., and Baron, M., eds., New York: Gardner Press, 1988.
The Hidden Child by Simmons, J. Rockville, MD: Woodbine House, 1987
Autism : Information and Resources for Parents, Families, and Professionals by Simpson, R., and Zionts, P., Austin, TX: PRO-ED, 1992
A Guide to Successful Employment for Individuals with Autism by Smith, M., Belcher, R., and Juhrs, P., Baltimore: Paul H. Brookes Publishing Co., 1995

Autobiographies of people dealing with autism
There's a Boy in Here, by Barron, J., and Barron, S. New York: Simon and Schuster, 1992
Thinking In Pictures and Other Reports From My Life with Autism by Grandin, T. New York: Doubleday, 1995
Emergence: Labeled Autistic by Grandin, T. Novato, CA: Arena Press, 1986
Without Reason: A Family Copes with Two Generations of Autism by Hart, C. New York: Harper & Row, 1989
Let Me Hear Your Voice; A Family's Triumph over Autism by Maurice, C. New York: Knopf, 1993
I Hope Some Lass Will Want Me After Reading All This by Miedzianik, D., Nottingham England: Nottingham University, 1986
The Siege by Park, C., New York: Harcourt, Brace, World, 1967
Somebody Somewhere by Williams, D. New York: Times Books, 1999

See also chart on page 14 for more about autism.

Chapter Twenty Five

Adapting Materials for Special Situations

- Do not be afraid to read to your student, either alternate paragraphs or entire sections.

- Whenever possible allow your student an alternative way to show that he has learned, such as doing a project, taking a test orally, making and labeling a map or diagram, making a scrapbook, creating a song, teaching another child, or making a working model.

- If educational movies are available on the subject, show them as introduction or summary.

- Allow your student to give oral answers to section or chapter summaries.

- Allow your student to read the review questions **before** he reads the text.

- Only require half as many responses. (Answer odd number questions, do section B, etc.)

- Allow your student to sit near you as he works.

- Allow your student to work in a private quiet room with no distractions. (A must for some.)

- Read the text to your student and tape record it to allow him to listen again.

- Outline the chapter for your student.

- Provide an outline formed correctly with only a few key words for your student to finish.

- Highlight important information in text.

- Reduce the assignment to its barest essentials.

- Allow student to make (or you make) a visual aid to summarize important concepts.

- Incorporate movement into learning and memorizing whenever possible.

- Relate the subject to something that is important to the learner.

- Refer as much as possible to things the student already knows that are similar.

• Identify for your student the key concepts required to pass the test.

• Reward your student (a penny, an M&M candy, 1 minute free time, etc.) for each fact he learns or problem he completes.

• Break learning sessions into small segments.

• Provide frequent review in different ways.

• Cut an intimidating math paper into strips or sections and do them at different times of the day.

• Mechanically enlarge the page (reading or math)125% or more.

• For older students who must do "baby work," reduce the page to 50% or even 25%. It doesn't look so babyish!

• When reading is difficult, cover page with a blue overhead projector transparency (dull side up). Available at office supply store. Try other colors.

• Learn only the most important information in small chunks with frequent reviews.

• Let the student who has difficulty writing use numeral and letter stamps.

• Give student daily grade for oral participation to offset test grades.

• Give test orally.

• Give open book tests.

• Give the student additional time to complete assignments (lessen the number of things the student must study).

• Whenever possible use two to three senses in both teaching and evaluating.

• Picture books often include information through the fourth grade level. Use them to introduce, simplify, identify truly important information, and show simplified illustrations and diagrams. Often they contain enough information for a developmentally delayed child.

• Break the task into smaller steps and take a step a day while reviewing previous steps.

• Give the student opportunity to teach a younger student a skill or concept he has learned.

• Find a teenager who can teach the concept or skill. They often have more patience.

• Allow the use of colored paper, bright markers, fun pens, etc, when taking notes or making summaries.

• Allow use of calculator for math and electronic spelling dictionary for spelling.

• Allow use of an addition or multiplication matrix (cheat sheet).

• Allow list or file of commonly misspelled words.

• Write or tape each problem or question to a 3 x 5 card.

• Allow a scrapbook report with pictures, diagrams, and charts instead of a written report.

• Supply clearly printed notes of important concepts for study.

• Allow the student to recreate in miniature some aspect of his learning such as the location of the event, the habitat of an animal, etc.

• Pick a topic. Have everyone read through different books at many levels to discover something to share about the topic. Do a group project, summarize the information, and test all together.

• Alternate easy and hard tasks, written and listening exercises, active and quiet lessons.

• Encourage the student to highlight important information, jot notes in the book, and in other ways make it his own learning tool.

• Teach the student to look for bold headings which summarize.

• Teach keyboarding and word processing skills early and allow assignments to be done on computer.

• Teach the student memory aids such as arranging details in alphabetical order or making up an acronym, a song, a rhyme, or a poem.

• Cover the facing page with blank paper to reduce distraction.

• Make a portable study corral. (Or make one for each child.)
      Use three pieces of 1/4" plywood 15" high by 18" to 24" long.
      Drill three holes (top, bottom, and middle) along one side of two of them.
      Drill matching holes on both sides of the third.
      Use large notebook rings (available from an office supply store) to join the three pieces.
      Stand the corral on the desk surrounding the child and his work to limit visual distraction.
      You may call this his private office.

Bonus Box

My Favorite Books on ADD/ADHD

The Hyper Active Child, by Dr. Grant Martin • ISBN 0-89693-968-8 • Victor Books

How to Reach and Teach ADD/ADHD Children by Sandra F. Rief
ISBN 0-87628-413-6 • The Center for Applied Research in Education • West Nyack, NY 10995

Maybe You Know My Kid! A Parents' Guide to Identifying, Understanding and Helping Your Child with Attention-deficit Hyperactivity Disorder by Mary Fowler • ISBN 1-55972-209-6

The Myth of the A.D.D. Child, by Thomas Armstrong, Ph.D.
ISBN 0-452-27457-4 • a Plume Book

ADD Quick Tips, by Crutsinger and Moore
ISBN 0-944662-05-6 • BRAINWORKS

Chapter Twenty Six

Testing

The topic of testing is dear to the heart of every person who deals with children - particularly children with special needs. Let me offer my particular perspective on this issue.

I am not in favor of testing in order to label. Learning problems do not generally have a medical cause which must be determined and treated in order to lessen or eliminate the difficulty. In my experience as a classroom teacher, I referred a child for testing in order to get him "identified" so that he could be placed in my care for help. It was a necessary part of the system. He could receive no additional help until some expert had determined that he fit the qualifications someone had established. If he did not fit someone's definition of some particular brand of "disability," he could not receive any special attention. A team of experts shifted the child around for a series of "evaluations," all of which were performed on one day in a hospital type setting. They reviewed statements from the parents and involved school personnel. Then a meeting was held and a written report was received. The results were consistently of two varieties: either the report told me in fancy terms exactly what I had told them, or the report described some child I had never met and I knew the child had not developed rapport with the situation (had been ill, uncomfortable, out of sorts, or frightened). Occasionally there were some suggestions I hadn't thought of, but in general the trauma caused by the situation was rarely worth the time and money spent.

On the other hand, almost everything I did every day was a test. Every time I asked the child for a response of any kind, I was evaluating what he had learned, and what I needed to present yet another time in a different way.

What is the difference? I believe it is related to II Corinthians 10:12b: "But they measuring themselves by themselves, and comparing themselves among themselves, are not wise." The tests performed by the "experts" were comparing children to other children. The tests I gave informally and frequently were comparing them to a standard. I believe there is a fundamental difference.

There are basically two different types of tests. One is the "norm" referenced test. It compares the student's response with other children in his category (age, grade, etc.). The results of a norm referenced test are reported in terms of percentile*, stanine*, mean*, or grade equivalent.*. The second type of test is a "criterion" referenced test. It determines what information a child has learned or what skills have been mastered. Its results may be reported in terms of percent of information learned, or statement of skills mastered.

*All averages or representative figures.

An example of the difference: The same test may be given in each. The difference is in what you do with and how you state the information you receive. You ask a kindergarten child to name the letters he sees. You list the letters he knows verses the letters he needs to work on. That is criterion reference. You state that he scores in the 90th percentile (meaning that only ten percent of children his age or in his grade usually score higher). That is norm referenced. You still don't know how many letters he needs to learn or which ones he knows.

What possible good can come from knowing that your child is in the 90th or the 10th percentile? You will either get an exalted picture of your child which may lead to still higher expectations and more academic pressure, or you will be discouraged and find the struggle even harder. The fact is, that by the very nature of this type of test, **someone** has to score in the top 10% and someone in the bottom 90% because children are being compared with each other. The results of this "norm referenced test" are stated in terms of percentile, mean, stanine, or grade equivalent.

The same is true of the concept of grades, A, B, C, D, and F. They are generally a comparison, not with a standard, but with a group. At one time, reaching a certain percentage of mastery determined the grade. All those who scored 95% or higher got A, etc. Gradually that has given way to a practice called grading on a curve. So many of the children get A's, so many get B's, etc. With this system, no matter what the ability of the students, no matter how well the teacher taught, a certain percentage of the class will get A and a certain percentage will get F. Another problem with grades is that there is no standard from class to class, from school to school, or from state to state. A student who earns an A in fifth grade English in Mississippi will not have learned the same information as a student in Iowa. How useful is this type of grade?

The testing which is helpful determines, instead, what the child had learned and what he needs to cover again. The evaluation needs to be diagnostic (helps you determine what your child doesn't know) and prescriptive (gives you what you need to teach missing skills). It is also best if incorporated casually into the normal course of the day and not isolated into a formal, highly stressful, and unfamiliar setting. If you are cooking dinner, you are constantly evaluating: Did I put in enough salt? Will the potatoes be done at the same time as the meat? The same thing should be happening in the classroom: Is she now able to print her name legibly? Has he really learned the parts of a flower? Can she apply the information about adding fractions? Every response is a test. It is not necessary to formalize and standardize the setting or the results.

I also want to comment on the current practice of "teaching to the test." When I began teaching 30 years ago, it was considered unethical to teach to the test (speaking of achievement tests). There is nothing wrong with teaching a child how to take a test by giving some sample problems in the same format of the test. There is, however, something wrong in knowing what the test will cover and teaching only that information. That practice is poor enough when used with text books, but inexcusable when looking at achievement tests.

Realistically, I understand that there will be circumstances where children must face standardized achievement tests and labeling in order to receive some special services or considerations within the system, but personally I believe that this should be avoided if at all possible. I believe I personally could refuse to cooperate with standardized testing on the basis of II Corinthians 10:12b and religious conviction.

Chapter Twenty Seven

General Resources

Additional Materials Evaluated by Joyce Herzog:

The author has evaluated over 500 and approved 200 additional materials for special needs children. This includes informative books and booklets on each area of special education, teaching job skills, and so on. The results of this research and many other items, such as information on teaching science related to the six creation days, have been published in the "Always Incomplete Resource Guide and Catalog."

> **Lifetime Books and Gifts**
> 3900 Chalet Suzanne Drive • Lake Wales, FL 33853
> www.lifetimeonline.com
> 1-863-676-6311 or *for orders only* 800-377-0390

For more thorough descriptions of many curriculum products, consult:
> *Christian Home Educator's Curriculum Manual,* by Cathy Duffy
> Both elementary and high school versions are available.
> <u>**Home Run Enterprises**</u>
> 12531 Aristocrat Ave.
> Garden Grove, CA 92614

These catalogs are informative and may prove very helpful in educating you as to what is available – and what is possible. Request catalogs from any companies which address topics you may be addressing with your children. But remember: It costs money to produce this material. Many of these companies are small and family-owned. Do not be overly generous with their advertising dollars.

If your student is old enough and able, have him write for these catalogs, or at least address the envelope! This is real, meaningful language arts and he'll be delighted when the catalog comes in his own name! Think of ways to involve your child in many such real-life educational opportunities. Many towns have excellent school supply stores and specialty children's toy shops. Look them over! When learning is fun, everyone is happy! Don't forget zoos and museums and summer recreational programs. They usually provide educational opportunities for all ages!

General Resources

ABC School Supply, Inc
3312 N Berkeley Lake Road • P.O. Box 100019 • Duluth, GA, 30136
Huge catalog of general supplies for children and learning.

ABeka Book
Pensacola, FL 32423-9160
800-874-2352
This company provides a complete textbook curriculum for grades kindergarten through high school. They emphasize memorization of facts through rote drill.

Academic Therapy Publications
20 Commercial Blvd. • Novato, CA 94949-6191 • 415-883-3314 • FAX 415-833-3720
800-422-7249 • http://www.atpub.com
> *Developing Your Child for Success* by Kenneth Lane
> *Vision Exercises* by Dr. Joel N. Zaba
> *Casebeer Program* by Beverly Casebeer
> *High Noon Books*
> *Ann Arbor Tracking Series*
> tests and many other books for special needs

A.C.E. (Accelerated Christian Education) School of Tomorrow
P.O. Box 1438 • Lewisville, TX 75067-1438
800-876-6176
K-12 worktexts (12 per subject per year), diagnostic, no parent preparation or involvement, much drill, simple recall rather than thinking.

Acorn Hill Cards for Kids
25440 Holly Ridge Road • Yadkinville, NC 27055 • 336-4169
Educational cards and collecting supplies, lesson ideas. Great supplement to any study – Bible, history, science. Children love to collect cards. Can be used as incentives or rewards. Please send SASE for description and price list.

Albert Whitman and Co.
5340 Oakton St. • Morton Grove, IL 60053 • 1-708-581-0033
Picture books for and about special needs children

AlphaOmega LifePac
P.O. Box 3153 • Tempe, AZ 85280
800-821-4443
Grades 1—12, diagnostic, uses parent involvement with activities plus independent work.

Alta Vista Curriculum
12324 Road 37 •Madera, CA 93638 • 599-645-4083 • 800-544-1397
Detailed, step by step units for PreK-9th grade, emphasis on learning to observe, think, and evaluate.

Always Incomplete Catalog and Resource Guide
Lifetime Books and Gifts • 3900 Chalet Suzanne Drive • Lake Wales FL 33853-7763
1-813-676-6311 or *for orders only* 800-377-0390
http://www.lifetimeonline.com
This catalog is a resource in itself. It includes extensive introductions to teaching plus descriptions of thousands of books. I have written introductions to each area of special needs and reviewed and described over two hundred special needs publications.

American Foundation for Blind
15 W. 16th St. • New York, NY 10011 • 1-212-620-2000
Parenting PreSchoolers, Excellent starter booklet for blind or vision-limited young child.

American Guidance Service (AGS®)
4201 Woodland Road • P.O. Box 99 • Circle Pines, MN 55014
800-328-2560 • www.agsnet.com
If you want junior and senior high school materials at a lower reading level, here they are. This secular company has lower reading level materials for math, grammar, writing, history, geography, science, citizenship, work, career, and life skills. It is also the source for the testing/assessment materials used by the schools and a variety of resources to "teach to the test."

American Teaching Aids
800-526-9907
Games, Charts, ReMark It Cards, Drill Workbooks (secular) and more! Look for the new Press and Check Cards - body heat reveals the answer! Can be used over and over.

The Arc of the United States
1010 Wayne Ave., Suite 650 • Silver Spring, MD 20910 • 301-565-3842 • Fax: 301-565-5342
Info@thearc.org
Picture cookbook, housekeeping checklist, apartment inventory, grooming skills designed for mentally retarded teenagers, much more.

Art Extension Press
P.O. Box 389 • Westport, CT 06881 • 203-256-9920 • FAX 203-259-8160
www.home-school.com/Mail/Artext
Source for small, inexpensive four-color reproductions of world masterpieces.

Attainment Company, Inc.
P.O. Box 930160 • Verona, WI 53593-0160
800-327-4269
Features life and survival skills, money, software for early childhood education, communication skills through pictures and a Pocket Talker™ (enables non-verbal to communicate with hearing world), and more.

Auditory Memory Publishing
2060 Raymond Ave. • Signal Hill, CA 90806
800-365-SING
Song cassettes available for teaching grammar, geography and math.

AVKO Educational Research Foundation
3084 W. Willard Road • Clio, MI 48420-7801 • 810-686-9283
Sequential Spelling allows students to correct their own mistakes, learn by practicing correctly, and build from simple pattern words to complex words. For instance, the words build from at to bat to batteries. Has worked with many children and adults.

Beautiful Feet Books
139 Main St. • Sandwich, MA 02563 • 508-833-8626
800-889-1978
Limited selection of quality books emphasizing literature, history and biographies.

Bluestocking Press
P.O. Box 2030 • Shingle Springs, CA 95682-2030
800-959-8586 • 530-621-1123 • FAX 530-642-9222
www.BluestockingPress.com
This company has the best selection of Easy Readers I've ever seen! Their resources for American history are excellent including historical documents, fiction, literature and non-fiction and the entire "Uncle Eric" series including, "Whatever Happened to Penny Candy?" and its two sequels. They also carry the Basic College Mathematics Series which they suggest can be started with adult assistance by 10-year-olds or by 12-year-olds for independent study. They suggest this is great for increasing morale of students with "math phobia."

Bob Jones Universtiy Press
Greenville, SC 29614
800-845-5731
This company provides a complete textbook curriculum for grades K- high school. Strong Biblical base, balanced teaching method, emphasize understanding of concepts, application of skills, and discernment in making choices.

Camp Venture & Co.
100 Convent Rd. • P.O. Box 402 • Nanuet, NY 10854
800-682-3714
Makes Dolly Downs™ (a doll that has Down Syndrome) and offers residential and day facilities.

Campus Co., Bill Weber
201 Jefferson Street • Stoughton, WI 53589 • 608-873-0404 • FAX 608-873-8494
EZFocus Portable Desk is a life-saver for your child who needs help focusing his attention on the job at hand! This little fold-up study carrel is made entirely of write-and-wipe surfaces and has many applications. A clip holds a pattern or paper right in front of the child - or a large rubber band even keeps his book open to the right page while he does his work. Optional side wings restrict distractions from the side. Optional speech mirror allows child to watch his own mouth as he practices articulation. Optional supports turn this into a slanted surface to assist children in developing writing skills. What a treasure and so inexpensive with so many uses! You and your children will love it!

Child's Work/Child's Play
135 Dupont Street • P.O. Box 760 • Plainview, NY 11803-0760
800-962-1141 • FAX 800-262-1886 • http://www.childswork.com • care@genesisdirect.com
Excellent (secular) books for all areas of special education plus marvelous games to teach skills like overcoming impulsivity, social communication, good behavior, and study skills. Your hardest job will be choosing which games to buy!

Christian Liberty Press
502 W. Euclid Ave. • Arlington Heights, IL 60004 • 708-259-8736
800-832-2141 • http://www.homeschools.org
Ministry providing eclectic collection of reprints and published materials which can be used as a correspondence school or purchased separately.

Christian Light
P.O. Box 1212 • Harrisonburg, VA 22801-1212 • 540-434-0768
Mennonite version of Alpha Omega's LifePacs plus some text books for science and history, carry wide line of supplementary materials, will work with learning disabled.

Christian Software Exclusive Manifold Marketing
4951 Mark John Way • Cumming GA 30130-6427
Christian software for reference, education, entertainment. Mostly IBM.

Color Historic America, Inc
Route 8, Box 922 • Cumming, GA 30130 • 404-889-6516
Coloring books for states and capitals and more.

Common Sense Press
8786 Highway 21 • Melrose, FL 32666 • 352-475-5757 • FAX 352-475-6105
http://www.cpress.com • service@cspress.com
Books and materials to enhance the Applied Approach to homeschooling such as: *Great Editing Adventure Series, Wordsmith, The Unit Study Idea Book* and *Creating Books with Children*

Concepts to Go
510-848-3233
Teaching Kits for math, language, visual perception and manipulative toys.

Conover Company Survival Skills System
1050 Witzel Ave. • Oshkosh, WI 54901
800-933-1933
Supplies for basic, survival, and vocational skills for severely handicapped.

Consumer Care Products, Inc.
PO Box 684 • Sheboygan, WI 53082 • 414-459-8353
Adaptive devices such as physically handicapped seats, stands, etc.

Continental Press
Elizabeth, PA 17022-2299
Report writing, workbooks.

Cornerstones Curriculum
2006 Flat Creek Place • Richardson, TX 75080
972-235-5149
Teaching a Christian worldview through math, science, history, and art.

Creative Publications
5040 West 111th Street • Oak Lawn, IL 60453
800-624-0822
Mathematics Their Way (activity based math) with counters and manipulatives of all kinds (bolts, pebbles, dinosaurs, toys, etc.) plus Jobcards™ (pre-made task cards) for developing all kinds of math and language skills and materials for thinking through math story problems.

Creative Teaching Associates
P.O. Box 7766 • Fresno, CA 93747 • FAX 209-291-2953
800-767-4282 • EMAIL: CTA@psnw.com
Games for Geography/History, Patterning & Spatial Relationships, Math, Language & Phonics, Science, and Bible. AIMS books and lab kits for teaching science through exploration.

Critical Thinking Press & Software
P.O. Box 448 • Pacific Grove, CA 93950
800-458-4849
Critical thinking books and computer software.

Cuisenaire Co. of America, Inc
P.O. Box 5026 • White Plains, NY 10602-5026
Mathematics Their Way emphasizes learning math concepts through hands on activities. Also source for all Cuisenaire rod materials and instruction as well as other math related products.

Curriculum Associates
800-225-0248
Brigance and other tests/materials used by special education teachers.

Demco's Kids Things
P.O. Box 7488 • Madison, WI 53707-7767
800-356-1200
Wonderful source for stuffed animals and puppets to correspond with most or your favorite picture books, like Madeline, Clifford the Big Red Dog. Also carries Brain Quest™ Curriculum Game which has illustrated questions (300 to 1500 depending on grade level) with answers for preschool through grade 7. Secular, carries books about witches and monsters as well. Also has big catalog with everything a school ever wanted!

Didax Educational Services
One Centennial Drive • Peabody, MA 01960
Manipulatives, puzzles, educational games and materials.

Different Roads to Learning
12 W. 18th St, Suite 3E • NY, NY 10011
800-853-1057 • Fax 800-317-9146
http://www.difflearn.com
Specializes in learning materials and playthings for children with developmental delays and challenges. This catalog puts together educational toys and materials that stimulate the skills leading to speech and language for challenged children ages 2 to 10.

Dinah Zike, Dinah-Might Activities
P.O. Box 690328 • San Antonio, TX 78269
Phone Orders Only: 800-99DINAH • 210-698-0123 • FAX 210-698-0095
http://www.dinah.com • Email: cecile@dinah.com
Where do I start? Getting reluctant learners to write! Using paper effectively! Making all kinds of books and projects! Extending hands-on learning into the content areas and up through high school and college! Dinah Zike will help you do all of this and more! Great resources for making learning come alive through involvement. For all ages and subjects! This is a MUST!

DLM Teaching Resources
Macmillan/McGraw-Hill • P.O. Box 543 • Blacklick, OH 43004-0543
800-843-8855
Software, early childhood, language, manipulatives.

Doorposts
5840 SW Old Hwy 47 Gaston, OR 97119 • 503-357-4749
www.lyonscom.com/Doorposts • doorposts@lyonscom.com
Disciplining and training children according to the Scripture is what these folks are all about. *For Instruction In Righteousnes* (Scriptures and suggestions for disciplining children), *Plants Grown Up* (Projects to lead boys to manhood), *Polished Cornerstones* (projects to lead girls to womanhood), *If Then and Blessing Charts* and more.

Dover Publications
Dept. CHS900 • 31 East 2nd Street • Mineola, NY 11501-3599
Nearly 2000 storybooks, coloring books, stencils and more – most $1.00 to $3.95. Ask for the Children's Book Catalog.

Dyslexic Reader
1601 Old Bayshore Hwy. #245 • Burlingame, CA 94010 • 650-692-7141 • FAX 650-692-7705
www.dyslexia.com
Newsletter for people experiencing difficulty learning to read. Related to Ron Davis's book, *The Gift of Dsyslexia*. Helpful hints plus advertising for their training program.

E21 Inc. Education for the 21ˢᵗ Century
P.O. Box 6481 • Chesapeake, VA 23323
800-440-8741
Career guidance including interest and personality assessment and information on more than 250 careers covering over 100 million jobs.

Ebsco Curriculum Materials
Box 11542 • Birmingham, AL 35202-1542
800-633-8623
Has simplified classics.

Edmark Corp
P.O. Box 3218 • Redmond, WA 98073-3218
800-426-0856
Learning Disabilities Resources, curriculum, deaf education including *Reading Milestones*, a highly recommended program for teaching reading through fourth grade to the hearing impaired. Touch Window for Apple and IBM compatibles!

Educational Resources
10200 W. 75th St. • Shawnee Mission, KS
Computer Software appropriate for special needs such as:

Clock	*Fast Track Fractions!*
Math Blaster Plus!	*Math Rabbit*
Race Car 'Rithmetic	*Spell It* (grades 1-6)
That's My Story!	*Writer Rabbit*
Stickybear , Numbers, Opposites and *Reading Comprehension*	

Educational Toys, Inc
P.O. Box 630882 • Miami, FL 33163-0882
800-881-1800
Miniaturized dinosaurs and sharks, enlarged insects, museum quality models, toys and games at reasonable prices.

Educators Publishers Service (EPS)
31 Smith Place • Cambridge, MA 02138-1089 • 617-547-6706 • FAX 617-547-0412
800-225-5750 • www.epsbooks.com
Primarily reading and language arts materials, some math, for all ages including *Explode the Code and Wordly Wise*

Elijah Company, Chris and Ellyn Davis
1053 Eldridge Loop • Crossville, TN 38558 • FAX 1-615-456-6384
1-888-2-ELIJAH • www.elijahco.com
This catalog is a resource in itself. Ellen Davis, author, teaches different curriculum approaches, science through nature study, wonderful history books, and more. Don't miss this one, but please order from them or they will have no reason to continue producing the catalog!

Essential Learning Products (ELP) Division of Teacher's Publishing /Highlights Company
2300 W. 5th Ave. • Columbus, OH 43216-2590 • 1-614-486-0633
Prime Time Library (Good Low-Vocabulary, Hi-Interest books for older delayed readers which are available with or without cassette accompaniment! *Developing Reading Power, Zaner-Bloser Handwriting Supplies*, and *Alphabet Desk Strips, Puzzle Books*

Exceptional Teaching Aids, Inc.
20102 Woodbine Ave. • Castro Valley, CA 94546-4232 • 510-582-4859
800-549-6999 • www.exceptionalteaching.com
Braille blocks for young children to learn the alphabet and Braille at the same time (safe for age 2 and up). Counting books, quiet books, Mangold Developmental Programs of Tactile Perception, Phonics ProReader™, math and reading, Menu Math, Work Jobs, textured dominoes, Braille playing cards, tactile dice, large print beginning readers, language, listening, social skills, parent resources, idea exchange and more. Great for anyone, including special needs.

Family Learning Connection, Mark and Janice Vreeland and Family
1934 South 56th Street • West Allis, WI 53219 • 414-327-4288
http://www.ameritech.net/users/familylearning/familylearn.html
Games, games, games! For every subject at every level! Inexpensive! This family of twelve creates and produces the games, provides workshops on developing games, and provides special music for churches and meetings when they are in the area. A wonderful resource!

Farm Country General Store
412 North Fork Road • Metamora, IL 61548
800-551-FARM • FAX orders: 1-309-367-2844 • All other calls: 1-309-367-2844
http://www.homeschoolfcgs.com • Email: fcgs@homeschoolfcgs.com
General homeschool supply company.

Five in a Row Publishing
14901 Pineview Dr • Grandview, MO 64030-4509 • 816-331-5769
http://www.fiveinarow.com
Preschool and elementary curriculum based on reading a picture book five days in a row and jumping from there into activities in language arts, math, history, geography, etc. *Five In A Row Holiday Book* gives origin, reminiscing and suggestions for crafts, books and activities for major holidays. Christian content.

Franklin Learning Resources
One Franklin Plaza • Burlington, NJ 08016-4907
800-525-9673 • FAX 609-387-1787
Spelling computers, computer aids in dictionary skills, languages and grammar.

Gallaudet Bookstore Catalog.
800 Florida Ave. • Washington DC 2002 • 202-651-5380
Materials for the hearing impaired

Gamco

P.O. Box 310F6 • Big Spring, TX 79721
800-351-1404
Computer programs for all areas of special needs and all subjects, including basic keyboard.

Gilford Press

72 Spring Stree •, New York, NY 10012
When Slow is Fast Enough Parenting Preschool Special Needs

Globe/Fearon Publishers

4350 Equity Drive • Columbus, OH 43228
800-877-4283 Ext.126
These people *sell only to schools* . To order from them, your homeschool must have a school name. When you call for a catalog, be ready to give the **name of your school**! It may also help to order under an invoice number. Any number will do. They have some wonderful materials for special needs. My favorites were: Fearon's *Our Century Magazines*. Nine softcover texts which cover the 1900's one decade at a time. Readability level is 3.5-4.5. Interest level is 6-12.
> *Biographies from American History* 30 Softcover books 2.5/ . 6-12)
> *World History Makers* 3 Softcover books (1.8/ 6-12)
> Fearon's *Amazing Adventures* 8 Novels (3.5/ 6-12)
> *Spell It Out* four-volume spelling, reading, writing, critical thinking (4.7/ 6-12)
> *Survival Vocabularies* Banking, driver's license, job applications, etc. (3.0 6-12)
> *Science In Action* Texts or Worktexts Life, Physical, and Earth Science (2.5-4./6-12)
> *Biology* Human, Plants and Animals) with Lab books. Free teacher's guide (2.5/ 6-12)
> *Mathematics Workshop:* Basic Skills, Problem Solving and Word Problems

Greenleaf Press, Rob and Cyndy Shearer

3761 Highway 109 N. Unit D • Lebanon, TN 37087 • FAX 615-449-4018
800-311-1508 • Customer Service: 1-615-559-1617 • www.greenleafpress.com
This catalog concentrates on the teaching of history through real books. Rob and Cyndy have republished some older books and written the "Greenleaf Guides" to several periods of history.

Hands On and Beyond

4813 East Marshall Drive • Vestal, NY 13850 • 607-722-6563
1-888-20-LEARN •http://www.handsonandbeyond.com
Hands on materials for history, science, math and more. Games for many periods of history and science topics. Construction sets, puzzles... Your "hands-on" learner will love you!

Hands On History

201 Constance Drive • New Lenox, IL 60451
Read about, dress up like, make authentic crafts of the period. More! Living History

Hands On Learning

417 Haines Ave. •Fairbanks, AK • 907-456-8356
"If I can build it, I can understand it." Materials for hands-on learners.

Hewitt Research Foundation

P.O. Box 9 Washougal, WA 98671-0009 • 360-835-8708
800-348-1750
Helps special needs families set up IEP, provides phone counseling, curriculum guidance, written evaluations, and more.

Highlights Catalog

2300 Hidden Picture Drive • P.O. Box 1450 Columbus, OH 43216-1450
800-422-6202 • www.highlightscatalog.com
We've all seen the magazines –in the doctor's office and around town – but did you know that they have a catalog of wonderful learning tools? Check this out before gift-giving occasions!

Home Computer Market

P.O. 385377 • Bloomington, MN 55438 • 612-866-4419
800-8277420 • www.homecomputermarket.com • email: themarket@usinternet.com
Carefully chosen computer resources for all ages.

How Great Thou Art

P.O. Box 48 • McFarlan, NC 28102 • 800-982-DRAW
Godly art curriculum for ages 5 and up, ties in with history.

The Homeschool Guide

Homeschool Advisor • 10424 Ewing Road • Bloomington, MN 55431
www.homeschooladvisor.com
Don't you wish someone would research and pre-screen computer programs and tell you which ones were good for what? Tammy and Dan Kihlstadius have done just that... **and tell** you how to choose a computer, whether to upgrade or replace/ tips for the internet, extensive list of software to avoid, tips for special needs and (nearly) frustration free computing and more!

HomeQuest

Local Independent Distributors 904-285-4699
800-473-9028
K-8th grade Computer curriculum which can be purchased or leased, in part or in entirety. Increases interest and success and allows student to work at his own pace with inter-active lessons. Includes use of human voices, music and animation. Though I do not believe any child should get their entire curriculum from a computer, it can be very helpful in interesting and assisting children in their weak areas.

IMED Publisher

1520 Cotner Avenue • Los Angeles, CA 90025
Multi-sensory learning materials.

Incentives for Learning, Inc

111 Center Ave,. Suite 1 • Pacheco, CA 94553 • 510-682-2428 • 510-682-2645
High interest/low reading ability, reading comprehension, read-along books, easy classics, *Ten-Minute Mysteries,* learning games at all levels for all topics.

Jesana Ltd.
PO Box 17 • Irvington, NY 10533
800-443-4728
Large print books, adapted toys and devices for physically handicapped, etc.

Joyce Herzog.com
800-745-8212 • www.joyceherzog.com
No resource list would be complete without mentioning my own web site and products.

Key Curriculum Press
2512 Martin Luther King Jr. Way • PO Box 2304 • Berkeley, CA, 94702
800-338-7638 • Fax 800-541-2442
Finally a source for special needs math at the junior high and high school level! Excellent, colorful, hands on, inexpensive materials for geometry, algebra, problem solving and more!

Konos Character Curriculum
P.O. Box 1534 • Richardson, TX 75083 • 214-669-8337
Very interactive unit study curriculum based on character traits for K-12, non sequential history

Lakeshore Learning Materials
2695 E Dominguez St. • Carson, CA 90749 • 310-537-8600 • FAX 310-537-5403
800-421-5354 • www.lakeshorelearning.com
Fabulous, fascinating learning tools! My favorites (in the Early Learning Catalog) were the sight word stamps (see a picture, stamp the word), make-a-word picture puzzles. They also have a Grades 1-3 catalog featuring more hands-on tools and some worktexts and "Basics and Beyond' with high-level interest, low level reading workbooks/books for the older learners.

Laurie
P.O. Box F • Phillips-Avon, Maine 04966 • 207-639-2000 • FAX 207-639-3555
800 451-0520 • FAX 800-682-3555
Love those quiet rubber puzzles - more than you every knew about **and** they replace pieces!

Learning Potentials Publishers, Inc.
230 West Main Street • Lewisville, TX 75057 • 214-221-2564
800-437-7976
Developing Your Child for Success by Kenneth A. Lane. Additional workbooks: *Recognition of Reversals, Spelling Tracking, Visual Tracing, Visual Scanning,* and *Visual Memory*

Learning Resources
380 N. Fairway Drive • Vernon Hills, IL 60061
800-222-3909 • FAX 800-222-0249
Games, activities, learning tools to teach math, language, science, and early childhood.

Lekotek
National Library System • 2100 Ridge Avenue • Evanston, IL 60204 • 708-328-0001
Lending toys, educational materials and equipment for children with disabilities.

Love and Learning
P.O. Box 4088 • Dearborn, MI 48126 • 313-581-8436
Learning series to teach language, reading and comprehension skills to children with Down Syndrome through the combined use of audio tapes, video tapes, and books.

Mantle Ministries
228 Still Ridge • Bulverde, TX 78263 •
877-548-2327 • www.mantlemin.com • mantleministries@cs.com
These folks are reprinting a series of American History books where most words are one syllable and the rest are divided into syllables. Great for students who want to learn, but still struggle a bit with reading. These books are from a providential and Christian perspective.

Miller Pads and Paper, Randy and Renee Miller
2840 Neff Road • Boscobel,WI 53805 • 608-375-2181
These friendly folks sell pads of all kinds of paper for drawing, writing, painting, and more at very reasonable prices. Try the 1" graph paper for your beginning printer who cannot print those capital letters on the line. When he is ready for lower case letters, try the 1/2" graph paper. 1/2" graph paper is also wonderful for keeping arithmetic problems in line from adding through long division. You'll be amazed at how this paper simplifies things! They also carry wonderful colors of construction paper and marvelous tempera paints with special daubers that let you paint without brushes! Excellent for those children who have trouble controlling a brush.

Mindplay
Department SN71 • 160 W. Fort Lowell Road • Tucson, AZ 85705
800-221-7911
Software for special needs children, accommodates different skill levels, allows each to work independently and set the pace.

Modern Curriculum Press
13900 Prospect Road • Cleveland, OH 44136
800-321-3106
Simple workbooks for most subjects plus phonic readers.

Montessori N' Such
6687 McLean Dr. • McLean, VA 22101 • 703-205-0890
Specialized toys help toddlers learn skills they'll use for a lifetime! Beautiful miniature dishes make you want to try your hand at pouring and table setting and other real life jobs.

Morgan's
P.O. Box 2279 • Asheville, NC 28802-2279
800-452-2868
Huge catalog of school supplies of every type. Includes MathSafari®.

M.O.V.E. International
1300 17th Street • Bakersfield, CA 93301 •
800-397-6683 (MOVE) • http://www.move-international.org

M.O.V.E., International – continued
These people are having great success improving the lives of the severely handicapped by getting them up on their feet and step by step moving into walking. A great side effect has been increased language skills. Creators of the "gait-trainer." If you've been told your child would "never walk," look at this!

My Clothes Are Super
Tammy McMannus
201 Birch Street • North Branch, MN 55056 • 612-674-8513
800-395-8660
Clothing designed to allow for body jackets, braces, undergarments, tubes, and more.

Nature's Workshop
22777 State Road 119 • Goshen, IN 46526 • 219-534-2245
Publisher of *Nature's Friend Magazine* and source for lab and nature study materials

Old Fashioned Products, Al and Sue Schuler
4860 Burnt Mountain Rd. • Ellijay, GA 30540 • FAX: 1-706-635-7611 or -7672
800-962-8849 • EMAIL: muggins@ellijay.com
These folks are the creators of all those wonderful math games – from *Number Neighbors* for the younger set and *Muggins* to practice =, -, x, and ÷ facts and beyond. Their games make practice of math skills fun! Available in marbles format, or as "write and wipe" boards.

Pathfinder Services, Inc
P.O. Box 1001 • Huntington, IN 46750
www.pathginderservices.org/islands • 888-888-1150
Fraction Islands® are manipulatives which allow students to learn fractions on a geoboard.

Peterson's Colleges with Programs for Students with Learning Disabilities by Charles Mangrum II and Stephen Struchart • ISBN 1-560790400-3 • Peterson's, Princeton, NJ
This manual lists colleges which are designed for or have programs to assist students who learn differently.

PSI Life Skills
5221 McCullough • San Antonio, TX 79212
800-594-4263 • FAX 210-824-8055
Life skills and communication skills.

Robinson Curriculum
Oregon Institute of Science and Medicine
2251 Dick George Road • Cave Junction, OR 97532 • 541-592-4142
Children teach themselves (via C. D. ROM) grades 1 through 12. Includes hundreds of original sources including 1911 Encyclopedia Britannica (I paid $200 for my hard copy!), 1913 Noah Webster's Dictionary and more

Rod and Staff
Route 172 • Crockett, KY 41413 • 606-522-4348
Mennonite, Biblically based textbook series for grades 1 or 2 – 8.

Sensational Beginnings
P.O. Box 2009 • 987 Stewart Road • Monroe, MI 48167 • 800-444-2147
Wonderful learning tools, sports equipment, costumes and furniture for infant through age 8.

Simplified Curriculum
P.O. Box 896 • Mount Dora, FL 32757
800-414-4852
Workbook curriculum for K-8 including all subjects and Biblical attributes of God in three month segments. Unlike other workbook curricula, you purchase this by the grade level and assume that a child will move evenly through all the subjects.

Software Learning Network
200 Fallen Palm Dr. • Casselberry, FL 32707
Source for computer shareware for the MacIntosh Computer!

Soft Touch
4300 Stine Rd Suite 44 • Bakersfield, CA 93313 • 661-396-8676 • FAX 661-396-8760
877-763-8868 • http://www.funsoftware.com • Softouch@funsoftware.com
Products which will help you open the computer to all learners – IntelliKeys®, simple switch, cognitive development for severely impaired

Solutions for Integrating Church and Home
P.O. Box 630 • Lorton, VA 22199 • 703-455-7461 • FAX 704-440-9798
www.unitingchurchandhome.com • email: Solution77@sprynet.com
Ministry seeking to reconnect the church and home through resources, conventions and seminars.

Special Times
CDL, Inc. • 214 Third Ave. • Waltham, MA 02154
Computer programs appropriate for special needs children.

Sport Time
One Sportime Way • Atlanta, GA 30340 • 770-449-5700 • FAX 770-263-0897
800-283-5700 • FAX 800-845-1535
These folks have at least three catalogs - *Sportime, Abilitations,* and *ChimeTime*. Get them all for ideas, pictures and hard-to-find items. *Sportime* is for physical education, recreation, athletics, aquatics, dance and health for all ages. *Abilitations* is equipment for development and restoration of physical and mental ability through movement. It carries some wonderful hard to find items like a $10 book rest to put reading materials at a proper visual angle, The Talking Pen®, Steady Write to eliminate shaky writing, and much more. They carry School-Write tracing board/stencils of the entire alphabet in cursive or manuscript which allow the child to trace the letters with a pencil. *Chime Time* carries wonderful toys/teaching tools for the infant through lower elementary with everything from blocks, steps, mats, drama, and gymnastics. Look at these when you're buying for Christmas, birthday or even setting up a preschool!

SRA/Macmillan (McGraw-Hill)
800-843-8855
> *Barnell/Loft*
> *Practicing Comprehension*
> *Spectrum Mathematics*
> *Science Research & Associates (SRA)*

Steck-Vaughn Company
P.O. Box 690789 • Orlando, Fl 32819-9998
800-531-5015 • FAX 800-699-9459 • www.steck-vaughn.com
These people have produced numerous materials to make teaching special needs children easier. All materials are labeled to tell you what grade level they are for and what reading level they are written at. They have high interest/low vocabulary materials so that your junior or senior high school student can study grade level topics at a lower reading level. They carry phonics readers, early reading fiction and nonfiction, test taking preparation materials and reading comprehension materials. Their Language Skill Books focus on different areas of language (Vocabulary, Usage and Spelling; Nouns, Verbs, and Sentences; or Pronouns, Adjectives, Adverbs, and Paragraphs). Their Short Classics have easy to read presentations with "carefully controlled vocabulary while maintaining the style of the original authors."

Straight Edge
296 Court Street • Brooklyn, NY 11231
Maker of learning place mats including math, geography, languages, braille and sign – they are also available through many teacher supply companies and better toy stores.

Teaching the Infant with Down Syndrome and *Teaching Reading to Children with Down Syndrome: A Guide for Parents and Teachers* by Patricia Logan Oelwein
Woodbine House, 6510 Bells Mill Road, Bethesda, MD 20817 • 800-843-7323
Excellent books and techniques even for other special needs and different learners.

Tapestry
Books 'N Kids • 17923 Teri Drive • Derwood, MD 20855 • 301-947-5137
www.TapestryOfGrace.com • 800-705-7487
Unit study curriculum based on Scripture.

Therapro
225 Arlington St. • Framingham, MA 01701-8723 • 508-872-9494 • FAX 800-268-6624
800-257-5376 • http://www.theraproducts.com
Supplies to enable you to do your own therapy plus books on ADD, sensory integration, geriatric needs, self-injurious behavior, simplified crafts, and more!

Therapy Skill Builders (Now a division of The Psychological Corporation)
P.O. Box 839954 • San Antonio, TX 78283-3954
800-211-8378 • TDD 800-723-1318 • FAX 800-232-1223
Assessment and intervention for special needs - infant through adult. *Action Alphabet*, motor, mobility skills, sensory integration, head injuries, stroke, dementia, managing behavior, ADD.

The Teaching Company

7405 Alban Station Court Suite A 107 • Springfield, VA 22150 • 703-912-6404
800-TEACH-12 (800-832-2412) • FAX 703-912-7756 • www.teachco.com
Non-credit high school courses by video: Become a Super Star Student, Chemistry, basic math, geometry, Algebra 1 and 11, World History, Early American History

Timberdoodle Company

E 1510 Spencer Lake Rd • Shelton, WA 98584 • 360 426-0672
800-478-0672 • http://www.timberdoodle.com • email: mailbag@timberdoodle.com
General Homeschool supplies.

Tobin's Lab – Hands-On Science Materials for Families

P.O. Box 725 • Culpeper, VA 22701
800-522-4776 • www.tobinlab.com • mike@tobinlab.com
Christian homeschool family business provides science materials, kits, chemicals of all kinds in small quantities for individual use at inexpensive prices.

Toys for Special Children

385 Warburton Avenue • Hastings-on-Hudson, NY 10706
http://www.enablingdevices.com
Specially adapted toys, electronics, communication devices, etc.

*Trisms (Time Related Integrated Studies for Middle School)

1203 S. Delaware Place • Tulsa, OK 74104-4129 • 918-585-2778 or 918-491-6826
Integrates reading, vocabulary, language arts, science, history, geography, culture studies, math, and Bible around a timeline. Useful for 6-8th graders (Special Ed high school). Written by a homeschooling Mom. Includes Daily Lesson plans, tests, student worksheets and assignments, answer key, resource lists and more. Allows flexibility of student choices and multi-level teaching.

Visual Manna

P.O. Box 553 • Salem, MO 65560 • 573-729-2100
888-275-7309 • http://www.visualmanna.com
Linking art to core curriculum is the goal of these precious folks. Whether you are building a model of the Viking's ship, copying a master from the Renaissance, designing a puppet and writing a dialogue, inventing something modeled after daVinci's own inventions, or communicating spiritual lessons, art will make your curriculum come alive.

Weaver Curriculum

888-367-9871 • www.weaverinc.com
Unit study curriculum based on the Bible, separate programs for preschool-kindergarten and 1-6th grade, can be expanded to include grades 7-12

Whole Heart Ministries

P.O. Box 67 • Walnut Springs, TX 76690

www.wholeheart.org

A ministry committed to write and publish quality resources for nurture, discipleship and education in homes with a goal of raising wholehearted children.

Woodbine House, INC.

5615 Fisher's Lane • Rockville, MD 20852

800-843-7323

Excellent (secular) resources for all areas of special education including Downs, Fragile X, Tourette Syndrome, and autism.

Zaner-Bloser

1459 King Avenue • Columbus, OH 43216-6764

Special pens, paper and other materials to make handwriting easier.

Chapter Twenty Eight

Deaf Education Resources

Resources for Deaf and Hearing Impaired

Educating the deaf is so unique that it requires a special section of resources. I am not as experienced in working with the deaf and have copied this from the NATHHAN News Summer 1994. Used with permission. This issue features homeschooling the deaf, cued speech, and more. To obtain a copy, contact NATHHAN. Back issues are $3.75 including postage.

Gallaudet Bookstore Catalog

800 Florida Ave. NE • Washington DC 20002 • 800-451-1073
Materials for the hearing impaired for all subjects. Curriculum guides for teaching deaf children a variety of subjects such as health, social studies, mathematics, and a preschool guide.

NICD National Information Center on Deafness

800 Florida Ave NE • Washington, DC 20002 • 202-651-5051 or TTY (202) 651-5052
Write or call for their list of articles relating to teaching deaf children, deafness, and communication. There is a minimal charge for these publications.

National Association of Deaf

301-587-6282
Materials for the hearing impaired.

HOPE, Inc.

809 North 800 East • Logan, UT 84321 • 801-752-9533
Excellent deaf, blind and deaf/blind resource especially for the birth to pre-school aged child. Catalog of resources for understanding and interacting, in family centered intervention.

Modern Signs Press, Inc.

P.O. Bos 1181 • Los Alamitos, CA 90720 • 310-596-8548 TDD/FAX (310) 795-6614
Good source for **Signing Exact English**. They carry a variety of books and tapes.

NAD (National Association of the Deaf) Bookstore

814 Thayer Ave. • Silver Spring, MD 20910 • 301-587-6282
They offer a catalog of a variety of materials.

Occupational Hearing Services

800-222-EARS (800-222-3277)
Not recommended for children under age 10.

Quiet Bears

P.O. Box 6542 • Ventura, CA 92006 ℐ 805-647-0609
This is a huggable, washable, signing bear puppet.

Edmark

P.O. Box 3218 • Redmond, WA 98073
800-362-2890
Their Reading Milestones, a sight word type curriculum, was developed to teach hearing impaired children.

Exceptional Teaching Aids

20102 Woodbine Ave. • Castro Valley, CA 94546-4232 • 510-582-4859
800-549-6999 • www.exceptionalteaching.com
Teaching tools for blind, deaf and more.

John Tracy Clinic

800-522-4582
This is an educational center for children birth through age five who are deaf. There is no charge for this correspondence course. They also have a program for deaf/blind for any age.

Tripod Grapevine

2901 N. Keystone St • Burbank, CA 91504
800-352-8888
Provides updated information on a variety of subjects such as Cued Speech, lip reading, sign, and many other issues relating to teaching deaf children. Any questions? Give them a call!

Let's Sign Inc

203-2 Enchanted Parkway • Manchester, MO 63021 • 314-230-9823
Books, jewelry, and other items pertaining to sign language. Call and ask for their free catalog.

West Coast Cued Speech Programs Resource Center

348 Cernon Street, Suite D • Vacaville, CA 95688 • 707-448-4060
Information on Cued Speech which is lip-reading supplemented by clear visual clues for phonemes. Highly effective for improving language patterns and reading ability of the deaf. Also benefits some students with learning disabilities such as dyslexia.

Deaf Homeschool Network

Agie@ncn.com

Deaf Ministries List

EEARL2@aol.com

Chapter Twenty Nine

Blind Education Resources

American Foundation for Blind
15 W. 16th St. • New York, NY 10011 • 212-620-2000
Parenting PreSchoolers, Excellent starter booklet for blind or vision-limited young child.

Braille Institute
Orange County Center 527 North Dale Ave. • Anaheim, CA 92801

Braille Sharing Library/Lysia Schuck
1981 Eden Road • Mason, MI 48854-9255 • 517 • 676-4621, laschuck@juno.com
Collection of Braille curriculum available to homeschooling families. The list of available materials is on the Buy, Sell, Donate page of the website <Resources for Parents and Teachers of Blind Children>

Exceptional Teaching Aids
20102 Woodbine Ave. • Castro Valley, CA 94546-4232 • 510-582-4859
800-549-6999 • www.exceptionalteaching.com
Teaching tools for blind, deaf and more.

John Tracy Clinic
800-522-4582
This is an educational center for children birth through age five who are deaf. There is no charge for this correspondence course. They also have a program for deaf/blind for any age.

National Federation of the Blind
1800 Johnson Street • Baltimore, MD 21230 • 410-659-9314

Seedlings Braille Books for Children
800-777-8552

Xavier Society for the Blind
154 E. 23rd Street • New York, NY 10010-4595
A Funny Alphabet Book , (a 6" thick tactile activities and objects for the alphabet), plus spiritual reading materials and religious textbooks in braille for the visually impaired.

Bonus Box

Helpful Special Education Web Sites:

Wellington Academy http://www.wellingtonsquare.com/academy.htm	**Love at Home** http://www.loveathome.com/homeschool/reading.htm
Teacher Freebies http://www.teacherfreebies.com/home.asp	**Homeschool World (Mary Pride)** http://www.home-school.com/
Math Goodies http://www.mathgoodies.com/homeschool/	**Joyce Herzog** http://www.joyceherzog.com
Families for the Early Treatment of Autism http://www.feat.org	**National Alliance for Autism Research** http://www.naar.org
Homeschooling Kids With Disabilities http://www.members.tripod.com/~Maaja/index.htm	**Learning Disabilities Online** http:www.ldonline.org
Special Education Network http://www.schoolnet.ca/sne/friends.html	**ADD - Mining Company** http://add.miningco.com
Special Needs Resources http://www.geocities.com/Athens/8259/special.html	**Dyslexia** http://www.dyslexia.com/
Special Needs Web Ring http://www.webring.org/cgi-bin/webring?ring=spneed;list	**Christian AD(H)D** http://www.concentric.net/~haynes2/adhd.html
LD Page http://homepage.bushnell.net/~peanuts/learningd.html	**Autism Society of America** http://www.autism-society.org
Learning Disabled and Gifted http://members.aol.com/discanner/ld.html	**Autism Resources** http://www.autism-info.com
Dyslexia Institute http://www.connect.bt.com/CampusConnect/orgs/org12281/index.html	
Dyslexic/ADD http://www.capecod.net/~rbf/a_Dyslexia_ADD.html	

Chapter Thirty

Speech and Language Development Resources

American Speech-Language-Hearning Association
10801 Rockville Pike • Rockville, MD 20852-3279 • 301-897-5700
800-638-8255

Imaginart Communication Products
800-828-1376 • www.imaginart.com
Functional speech and language materials for infant through elderly.

Janelle Publications Creative Speech and Language Materials
P.O. Box 811 • 1189 Twombley Road • DeKalb, IL 60115
FAX 815-756-479 • www.janellepublications.com
Earobics®, BoardMaker® (communication display maker for nonverbal children), games,
activities, resources for testing, understanding and remediating speech and language difficulties.

Dr. Libby Kumin. Dr. Kumin addresses the pre-speech skills. She primarily addresses Down
Syndrome issues, but many of their needs, such as oral motor, apraxia and motor planning skills,
are common to other syndromes as well. She is quite knowledgeable and a great presenter. Her
book, *Communication Skills in Children with Down Syndrome - A Guide for Parents*, was
published by Woodbine House (see resource list).

Communication Skill Builders, a division of the Psychological Corporation
555 Academic Court • San Antonio, TX 78204-2498
800-228-0752 • FAX 800-232-1223 • TDD 800-723-1318
Materials for developing language at all levels from infancy through adult, articulation through
social usage, multiple disabilities such as self-talk for hearing and severe language impairments.

Crestwood Company
6625 N. Sidney Place • Milwaukee, WI 53209-3259
Materials to develop language and communication skills.

Laureate Learning Systems, Inc.
110 East Sprint St. • Winooski, VT 05404
800-562-6801
Sequential Software for Language intervention for special needs children.

LinguiSystems , Inc
3100 4th Avenue • East Moline, IL 61244-9700
800-PRO IDEA (800-776-4332)
This Speech and Language Catalog is heavily slanted toward worksheets and designed for professionals, but will be valuable for you to see what is available and being used.

PSI Life Skills
5221 McCullough • San Antonio, TX 79212
800-594-4263 • FAX 210-824-8055
Games, Software, Reference, workplace simulation, behavior training, communication aides for those who are nonverbal including audio cards, the Five Talker, picture files, and "Can't Wait to Communicate." For elementary through adult. These folks cover life skills from all directions! Check prices, though. Found one item at twice the price of a different supplier, so be careful!

Straight Talk, by Marisa Lapish
NATHHAN (NATional cHallenged Homeschoolers) • P.O. Box 39. • Porthill, ID • 208-267-6246 http://www.NATHHAN.com • NATHANEWS@aol.com
Straight Talk I is an excellent book and video set which enables you to correct your child's mispronounciations at home. *Straight Talk II* deals with language delays.

Super Duper Publications: Speech and Language Materials
P.O. Box 24997 • Greenville, SC 29616-2497 • FAX 800-978-7379
800-277-8737
If it has to do with speech or language, these folks have it: books, games, tools galore! Auditory processing, vocabulary building, sign language, sensory integration and more! Blank game-boards, computer programs, audio card equipment. Pictures and miniatures for every use you can think of! Language skills for babies - for social situations. These people know all those words: apraxia, aphasia, dysarthria and dysphagia. Even resources for rehabilitating stroke victims!

Scientific Learning Corporation
1995 University Avenue • Suite 400 • Berkeley, CA 94704
Phone: 1-888-665-9707 • Fax: 510.665.1717
http://www.scilearn.com • Email: info@scilearn.com
Fast ForWord®, is an interactive, computer-based training program that builds the fundamental language skills critical for reading success and communicating in and out of the classroom. This expensive {$850 for 6-8 weeks, 2 hours a day} program slows down language, teaches specific skills, then slowly rebuilds the speed. It must be administered by a trained professional. Other options are designed to evaluate and develop speech and reading skills. In addition, Scientific Learning's **BrainConnnection.com** is an online source for news and information about how the brain works, how people learn and how neuroscience discoveries from around the world relate to our daily lives.

American Speech-Language- Hearing Association
10801 Rockville Pike • Rockville, MD 208052-3279
800- 638-8255 or 301-897-5700

Chapter Thirty One

Legal Information, Special Needs Support Groups, Magazines

Legal Information

HSLDA **(Home School Legal Defense Association)**
P.O. Box 159 • Paeonian Springs, VA 22129 • 703-338-5600
Provides information packet for families who are educating special needs children including general information, curriculum sources, and other resources. Refers to consultants if needed. Puts out a bi-monthly newsletter and provides legal defense for members.

NICHCY (National Information Center for Children and Youth with Disabilities)
PO Box 1492 • Washington, D.C. 20013-1492
800-695-0285
Marvelous free fact sheets and informative up-to-date bulletins on specific topics as well as resources state by state.

Your local state or national homeschool organization.

Special Needs Support Groups

NATHHAN (NATional cHallenged Homeschoolers Association Network)
P.O. Box 39 • Porthill, ID 83853
www.NATHHAN.com • email: NATHANEWS@aol.com
A network for families homeschooling special needs children which connects you with another family, provides resources and an inspiring and informative newsletter.

C.H.A.D.D. (Children and Adults with Attention Deficit Disorders)
499 N.W. 70th Avenue • Suite 102 • Plantation, FL 33317 • 305-792-8944
Secular support organization with local groups all over the country for families dealing with ADD and ADHD. Produces semiannual magazine, monthly newsletter, and other resources.

Christian Cottage Schools
Mike and Terry Spray • 3560 West Dawson Road • Sedalia, CO 80135 • 303-688-6626
http://wwwchristiancottage.com
Testing and curriculum counseling. They have some great full year unit study curricula.

Cure Autism Now (CAN)
5225 Wilshire Boulevard • Suite 503 • Los Angeles, CA 90036 • 213-549-0500
Information exchange for families affected by autism. Founded by parents dedicated to finding effective biological treatments for autism. Sponsors talks, conferences, and research.

Joyce Herzog
www.joyceherzog.com • 800-745-8212
Encouragement, curriculum consultations, advice, resources. Ask for Phone Therapy Kit.

Hopes – Homeschooling Our Precious Exceptional Students
864-834-0264

Lighthouse Educational Services
1101 Fairway Drive • Clayton, NC 27520 • 919-876-3848 • 919-553-6417
lightedu@earthlink.net

National Parent to Parent Support and Information System, Inc. (NPPSIS)
P.O. Box 907 • Blue Ridge, GA 30513 • 706-374-3822 • Fax: 1-706-374-3826 • TDD Available
800-651-1151 (for parents) • nppsis@ellijay.com
Linking parents of children with special health care needs and rare disorders.

National Respite Locator Service (a program of the ARCH National Resource Center)
Chapel Hill Training-Outreach Project • 800 Eastowne Drive, Suite 105 • Chapel Hill, NC 27514
http://www.chtop.com/locator.htm
Finding respite care.

O.U.C.H. Ohio's Uniquely Challenged Homeschoolers
RCHOSEN@visn.net

PICC Parents Instructing Challenged Children
315-592-725 • http:www.oswego.edu/mulvey/picc.html

Shepherd Boy – Strategies for Autism
4241 Faye Drive • Olive Branch, MS 38654 • 662-893-0611
www.shepherdboy.org • CShepherdboy@cs.com
Shepherd Boy is designed to offer strategies for working with individuals with autism and related disabilites through a newsletter, curriculum, writing, consultation and speaking.

Specially Gifted c/o the Pegrams
804-323-1786

Magazines

Parent Resource Magazines

The Teaching Home
Box 20219 • Portland OR 97220
Issues June, July 1990 and July, August 1994 feature special education.
Magazine has articles to help both newcomers and old-timers in homeschooling.

Homeschooling Today
PO Box 1425 • Melrose, FL 32666
Features read-it-today, use-it-tomorrow articles.

Homeschool Digest
Wisdom Publications
P.O. Box 575 • Winona Lake, IN 46590
Informative articles and inspirational essays to expose homeschoolers to the wide scope of issues surrounding the homeschool movement.

Hearing Hearts
Mrs. Beverly Cox
4 Silo Court • Sterling, VA 20164
Quarterly gospel magazine for the deaf from American Ministries to the Deaf.

Just Allergies
2756 NE 97 Street • Seatle, WA 98115
A newsletter for parents of children challenged by allergies, sensitivities, and intolerances.

Keepers at Home Magazine
Carlisle Press • 2673 TR421 • Sugarcreek, OH 44681 • 330-852-1900 • FAX 330-852-3285
800-852-4482
Issued quarterly for mothers who stay at home. Includes some homeschooling tips, old-fashioned ways of doing things and encouragement.

PREACCH
Jill Bond 1960 E. Phillips Court • Merrit Island, FL 32952
Round-robin newsletter full of heart-warming letters from families with autistic children.

MYRRH
#197-919C Albert St. • Regina, SK Canada S4R 2P6
1-306-545-8017 (Fax 306-569-8649)
An interesting and informative newsletter for homeschooling families.

The Good News
The Good News • PO Box 54410 • Cincinnati, OH, 45254-9900
Six **free** thought-provoking issues a year – for children through adults.

Guideposts Magazine
P.O. Box 856, Carmel, NY 10512-0856
This fine magazine routinely includes stories of people who conquer insurmountable odds to succeed in life. These are wonderful read-alouds for encouraging troubled learners and keeping life's problems in perspective!

Magazines for Children

God's World News
P.O. Box 2330 • Asheville, NC 28802-2330 • 800-951-5437
26 issues mid-September through mid-May at four different grade levels PreK-9th grade or adult. News from a Christian perspective for all ages.

Boy's Quest and *Hopskotch for Girls*
 P.O. Box 164 • Bluffton, OH 45817 • 800-358-4732
Each issue on a different theme, supports family values, no advertising, violence, evolution or Halloween. Science, math, reading, drawing, history, puzzles, cooking, crafts and more.

Cobblestone Magazines
 7 School Street • Peterborough, NH 03458-1454 • 603-924-7209
800-821-0115
Four different magazines available for 4-9th graders: World History, World Cultures, American History, Science. (Secular)

Guideposts for Kids
16 East 34th St. NY, NY 10016 • FAX 914-228-2151
800-932-2145 • http://.www.guideposts.org
Recommended for ages 6-12.

Nature Friend Magazine
Carlisle Press • 2673 TR421 • Sugarcreek, OH 44681 • 330-852-1900 • FAX 330-852-3285
800-852-4482
Stories, news and experiments about nature and character, but no advertisements!

Ranger Rick Magazine
8925 Leesburg Pike • Vienna, VA 22184-0001 • 800-432-6564
Nature magazine for children.

Credits and Thanks

Tucked in the back corner – not because they are not important, but because I am not a skilled graphics person and the pages are already done! And perhaps it is symbolic of the behind-the-scenes positions these people humbly occupy so well.

How can I say thanks? Many people have been instumental in helping me make this book what it is. Where do I start?

Thanks to my husband for believing in me when there were only hopes and promises. I told you, "You ain't seen nothing yet!"

Thanks to Virginia and A who listen to me, pray for me, tell others about me and have become family.

Thanks to Josh and Cindy Wiggers for prayers, editing, encouragement and hope.

Thanks to Annette Barbee, Mrs. Average Homeschooler, who has become friend, advisor, co-author and consultant and a prayer warrior.

Thanks to Theresa Sykes, and her son Will who believe in me, pray for me, encourage me, and have awesome dreams for me and my materials. Thanks, too, Theresa, for your strict editing! I don't always like it, but I love it!

Thanks to Sharon Adams who follows me like a puppy dog and encourages me to reach for the stars.

Thanks to Joe and Jeanette for the many years of service which freed us to concentrate on what we do best.

Thanks to Jan and clan for the space to work, the freedom to live cheaply, and the belief that what I am doing counts.

Thanks to the birds outside my office window who go on about life and cheer me on even when nothing seems to be going forward – to the dogs who always rejoice at my coming – to the garden which brings me such peace and contentment.

Thanks to all of you "out there" who ask me questions, listen to my advice, and even take it sometimes. How you humble me! Thanks, especially, to those who share their stories when there's a minute free and let me know how God has used me or my products to be a blessing. Where would I be without you?

Thanks to God Who called me from the tiny third-story closet to this country office to do greater things. It is my prayer that I always give You the glory You deserve for making me what I am.